D1389616

700034336048

the butcher

the butcher

LEANNE KITCHEN

MURDOCH BOOKS

contents

introduction

For as long as humans have walked the earth, animals and birds have provided us with pelts, milk, horn, feathers, eggs and meat. Today, throughout the world, a host of creatures great and small — from the guinea pig to the donkey, horse, and even dog, crocodile, turtle and snake — are considered fair dining game. Generally, most of us in the West don't have access to such exotica and are most likely to prefer dining on more domesticated creatures such as beef, lamb, poultry, game or pork.

Ancient hunter-gatherers had to count on success with hunting to enjoy whatever meat they could get hold of — but once animals were domesticated, a more reliable supply was possible. In times past, our relationship to our sheep, cows, pigs and poultry was an immediate one, as households and farmers raised their own animals in a free-range, non-intensive environment, and slaughtered them seasonally, as needed, for food. Many larger animals were valued for their labour and were killed only when their useful life was over; fowl were culled once they stopped laying. From necessity, every part of a beast was used, ultimately yielding some of the world's most beloved 'peasant' dishes — for example brawn (made from the meat of a boiled pig's head), oxtail stew, the various blood sausages still consumed throughout Europe, and stuffed pig's trotters. What couldn't be immediately consumed was preserved in salt, fat or brine, or by curing, fermenting or smoking.

In whatever form it was served, meat was highly valued and very expensive — the land and fodder required to raise animals was not something most people could afford. Before refrigeration, meat was enjoyed in quantity only by the wealthy; the poor had to make do with what they could produce and often saved meat meals for special occasions and religious feast days. Fast-forward to the modern age, where the vast majority of First Worlders plop their (typically) plastic-wrapped trays of pre-portioned meat cuts into supermarket trolleys, where they jostle next to bottles of dishwashing detergent, tins of cat food, packs of snack food and cartons of milk. It's a sanitised exercise that speaks nothing of where the meat has come from, how it was reared and husbanded, or how it was killed and processed.

Truthfully, most of us would rather not remember that the meat on our plates once had beating hearts, cute faces and appealing eyes. We've become quite squeamish about such things — and our convenience-driven shopping habits aren't exactly helping, removing us further and further from the very sources of our foods. Foodstuffs — from cheese to chocolate to chicken — are now regarded as day-to-day commodities of equal value. It is unfortunate and sad that this trend includes meat, as its original suppliers ultimately give up their lives to provide it for us. To consider meat as just another item on the shopping list seems, somehow, to disrespect its sources.

It is ironic, too, that in this age of an easily accessed, seven-day-a-week meat supply, confusion reigns and debates rage. Is meat good for us, or bad? Doesn't it burst with life-shortening fats — and isn't much of it reared with the aid of growth hormones and antibiotics? How can one tell prime from poor-quality meat, and what makes meat sometimes go tough or dry when cooked? Is meat from the supermarket inferior to that from old-fashioned butchers, and what's all the fuss over grain-fed versus grass-fed beef and cooped-up versus free-range hens? What about organic meat — is it worth the higher prices it commands?

What is never in doubt is that meat, in moderation, is good for us — it is an excellent source of protein and, particularly in the case of red meat, iron and B vitamins. And, when treated respectfully and cooked appropriately, it is also utterly delicious.

When it comes to buying meat, there are many good reasons to patronise a dedicated, traditional meat retailer — in other words, a butcher. They can dispense free tips and information about the cuts they sell, advise how much you'll need and how to cook it. They should be able to tell you all about the meat you buy — how it was fed, how it was aged and how long it has been hung. They'll have made their own sausages and smallgoods from scratch and will order in something special for you if you ask them to. Above all, they will sell you good meat — and good meat is a revelation.

'Ordinary' meat (and our world is awash with it) is produced according to dubious principles such as cheapness, efficiency and consistency of supply, and is just, well, ordinary. We owe it to ourselves, and to the animals that provide it, to buy the best meat we possibly can, to cook it as carefully and as knowledgeably as we possibly can — and to really enjoy the difference.

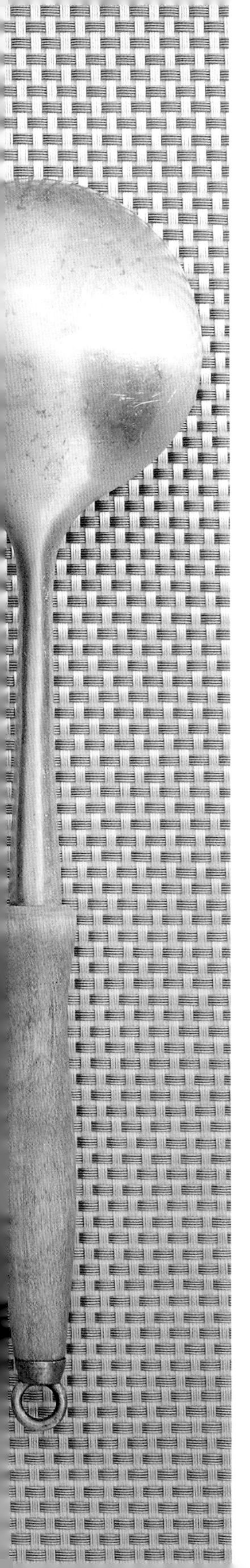

the basics

The world of meat cookery can seem complex and specialised, full of tricky techniques and expensive equipment. But really, the techniques amount to no more than a basic understanding of meat cuts and a few simple culinary rules — and you'll be amazed at what you can achieve with the kitchen cookware already sitting in your cupboards!

EQUIPMENT

ROASTING TINS

It is handy to have a selection of roasting tins, as roasts come in many different sizes — from chickens to whole turkeys. For successful roasting, it is vital to use a roasting tin that is neither too large nor too small. It is possible to buy 'covered roasters' which have deep sides and a lid, but cooking in one of these is really more 'pot-roasting' as meat steams when cooked under cover. Roasting tins are made from a number of materials; among the most popular are stainless steel, aluminium, copper, blue steel and enamelled steel. Non-stick roasting tins may be convenient, but they tend to stop pan juices browning; dark roasting tins also make it hard to see if pan juices are browning. A roasting tin should ideally be flameproof (so you can put it directly on the stove after the roast has cooked to make a gravy or jus); for this reason ceramic and glass roasting dishes should be avoided. A roasting tin should be fairly solid, so it won't warp under intense heat or weight, but not so heavy that it is unwieldy. It should have solid handles — the best types are upright handles that are firmly riveted in.

Roasting racks

These are wire contraptions that sit in the roasting tin; the meat is placed on the rack to cook. The rack lifts the meat off the roasting tin so the air can circulate freely and the roast can brown and cook evenly (without sticking to the pan). However, some cooks sit their meat directly in the roasting tin in the belief that they get tastier juices this way. Racks come in various shapes for various functions. There are flat ones, V-shaped ones (both adjustable and non-adjustable), basket racks, curved cradle-style racks and vertical poultry roasting racks. Usually roasting racks are made of stainless steel, and some are made with a non-stick surface that is far easier to clean than regular surfaces. The best racks are sturdy, with good handles for easy gripping so you can carry the cooked roast to a board for carving; some even come apart to facilitate cleaning. Make sure the rack will fit into your tin and that it will easily clear the top of the oven once you sit a roast or bird on it.

Basters

Basting a roast with the pan juices during cooking can add to its flavour and moistness. Many people no longer bother to baste but it is easily done. You can use a brush for this purpose — choose one with natural bristles and a long, sturdy shaft so you can stay a comfortable distance from the heat while you baste. Another option is a bulb baster, which resembles a giant eye-dropper and has a rubber bulb attached to the end of a metal or heat-resistant glass tube. Suction created when you press, then release, the bulb draws up pan juices and fat, then you simply squeeze the bulb to release the liquid over the meat. Glass ones are good because you can see how much liquid is in the baster — but make sure it is truly heat-resistant or it could shatter.

Lacers and trussing needles

Lacers are small metal skewers used to close the cavity of a stuffed bird. These are arranged around the cavity, secured by pinning them through the skin of the bird; the string is then threaded through an eyelet hole at one end and secured. Lacers should be quite strong (you don't want them to bend). Another way to close a cavity is to use a trussing needle and kitchen string. An advantage of a trussing needle over lacers is that you can properly truss the bird — secure the wings close to the body, tightly secure the legs and close the cavity — so it will keep a neat shape and cook through evenly. Trussing needles are made of stainless steel and have a sharp, flattened tip for piercing skin. Curved (rather than straight) needles are useful for tricky, hard-to-reach areas and also around bones.

Meat/carving fork

A good-quality fork is indispensable for meat cookery. It can be used for securing meat while carving, turning large pieces of meat or whole birds over during cooking, for removing large pieces to a board for carving, and general manoeuvring. They are about 30 cm (12 inches) long and made of forged stainless or carbon steel. The best-quality ones are very expensive, but have the best design and are the most durable. Some forks have curved prongs while others have straight — the straight sort are ideal for carving smaller pieces of meat (such as a chicken, duck breast or T-bone steak), while a curved fork is best for securing larger pieces of meat when carving.

Tongs

Tongs are like an extension of your arm and are used for turning meats over during cooking, lifting meats out of liquid, retrieving meats from marinades and so on. It is worth buying sturdy, good-quality ones. Spring-action tongs, which have a catch-closure that keeps the arms together when not in use, are the most effective. Longer ones are better when you want to avoid contact with intense heat, such as over a barbecue, but shorter ones do give you better control and are better for general use.

Ladles

You'll be using ladles a lot — to ladle sauces and soups for serving, and to skim fat and impurities from stocks. Avoid cheap, plastic ones and equip yourself with at least two top-quality stainless-steel ones of different sizes. They should be constructed from one piece of metal so there are no joins where bacteria can collect. For skimming, choose one with a smaller bowl. For serving soups, you'll need one with a large bowl. For serving sauces, especially if you wish to create a fine ribbon on the plate, choose a small one with a little rounded spout.

Spatulas

For flipping burgers, steaks or any pan-fried food, a spatula is very useful. Some are made from sophisticated heat-resistant plastics, others from metal. Some are quite rigid while others are flexible. Some are slotted and others are not. You need to assess what you will be most using your spatula for and which type feels most comfortable in your hand. (Metal spatulas can damage non-stick surfaces, so bear this in mind if you use non-stick tins.) The handles should be strong enough that they don't bend under weight, and long enough to keep your hands away from the heat. Perforated spatulas are good when there's fat or liquid to be drained from food.

Strainers and sieves

You'll need a strong, large strainer for straining stocks and a smaller, fine sieve for straining sauces for serving. The best sieve for meat cookery is a fine mesh chinois, or conical strainer. These come in many sizes and sit securely over bowls and saucepans thanks to a hooked bracket opposite their long handle; the fine mesh traps tiny solids and ensures a smooth texture for sauces. You can also buy a metal chinois with fine perforations instead of mesh, which is much easier to clean. For straining stocks, you don't need a very fine sieve — but you do need a well-made, large, strong one that can take the weight of heavy bones and vegetables. The rim needs to be strong too, so it won't warp with use, with rugged joins at the handle and hook.

Thermometers

Instant-read thermometers are brilliant for home cooks. You can buy dial models, where the temperature is shown by a needle on a classic round dial, or digital thermometers. The dial types display a smaller temperature range than digital ones and you need to insert them quite deeply into food for an accurate reading, so they are best used for large pieces of meat. Digital models are easier to read and more accurate, but are also more expensive. Some digital models are very sophisticated, allowing you to leave the probe in the meat for continuous temperature monitoring, and some even have alarms that alert you when the meat is cooked to your preference.

Knives

For meat cookery, the knives you'll most likely need are a large, general-purpose cook's knife, a boning knife, and a carving or slicing knife. Cook's knives are designed mainly for chopping, but can slice and dice as well. The most useful length is generally around 25 cm (10 inches). A good boning knife is essential — boning out a leg of lamb, a chicken breast or even a tiny quail is not terribly difficult with the right knife. Boning knives have a narrow, tapered blade (about 1.5 cm/5/8 inch wide) with a sharp, pointed end that manoeuvres easily and safely around bones and hard-to-reach places. The blades can be very bendy or absolutely rigid — generally, the larger the piece of meat, the more rigid the blade needs to be. Many people prefer a knife with a little 'give' in the blade for optimal versatility, so they can get by with just one boning knife. Slicing or carving knives have long, thin, tapered blades and vary greatly in their flexibility, their edge (some are smooth, some serrated) and their tips (rounded or pointed). Sharp-tipped knives are best for carving meats with bones, as the tip can be used to free meat from the bone; rounded ones are better for large boned meats. Flexible knives are best for poultry, and rigid ones for beef, pork or lamb. For larger pieces of meat you need at least a 25 cm (10 inch) blade, while a smaller one is perfect for smaller cuts like loins and fillets.

When choosing a knife, consider the blade material, handle design, weight and balance. A top-quality knife is a costly investment — but if cared for properly will never need replacing and will perform far better than cheaper alternatives. Knife handles can be made of stainless steel, wood and sophisticated plastic or rubber compounds. Choose a highly durable handle that has no joins or seams that are likely to harbour bugs or trap small bits of food. The tang of the knife — the part of the blade that extends into the handle — and the blade should all be forged from one piece of metal and ideally extend the whole length of the handle. Any rivets holding the tang in place should be smoothly flush with the handle. The length of the tang is what makes a knife strong and gives it balance. A blunt knife is dangerous because you need to exert undue pressure when cutting, which can cause you to slip and cut yourself, so invest in a good steel for maintaining the edge on your blades — you need to use the steel as often as you use your knives. Every time a sharpened blade comes into contact with a chopping board, the edge gets dulled. A steel will only maintain the edge — if a knife blade is completely blunt, have it sharpened professionally (it is very easy to ruin a knife through inexperienced sharpening).

Meat grinders/mincers

Meat grinders have been largely superseded by food processors, but still have their place. Food processors tend to mangle meat fibres, giving a more mushy, sticky result. A dedicated mincer instead cuts through the meat, giving a better texture. Mincers are also indispensable for sausage making, and useful too for mincing cooked, leftover meat for pies and other dishes. Relatively inexpensive manual grinders, which you clamp onto a bench or table, are still available and do a great job. They are heavy, made of plated cast iron, and work by a crank-handle operation, which forces the meat down a tube fitted with a large screw-like arrangement and through a grinding knife. They usually come with several changeable discs of varying fineness. Manual grinders are simple to use and very durable as not much can break or go wrong. The discs, screw and grinding blade must be very well washed and dried after use so they don't rust. Some standing cake mixers also have meat grinder attachments, but their efficiency depends on the strength of the machine's motor — if you have a powerful mixer, they're a good option. Often these attachments come with sausage-stuffing horns so you can make your own sausages easily. Free-standing, purpose-made electric grinders work in the same way. Choose one with the most powerful motor available, and for sturdiness, one with metal (rather than plastic) components.

Pounders

Escalopes, 'minute' steaks and sometimes chicken breasts can require pounding to flatten them. Pounders are not to be confused with meat mallets, which are designed to tenderise meat. Pounders are used solely to pound out meat to uniform thickness for even cooking, although the pounding process does also tenderise as it breaks down muscle fibres. Meat pounders must be heavy (around 900 g/2 lb) to be effective and have a smooth surface with no sharp edges. Some have a vertical design, like a coffee tamper, and require you to make stamping motions over the meat; others have a flat design with an off-set handle, and these require a slapping motion. Take care when using a mallet on any meat — strictly speaking, the way to deal with tough meat is to braise it, not mangle it with a mallet, which can cause precious moisture loss.

Chargrill pans

These are handy if you don't have a barbecue, or if it's inconvenient to barbecue. They are essentially a large, heavy-based skillet with raised ridges that leave their impression charred onto the food. They are best for small, tender cuts such as lamb cutlets, lamb eye fillets, chicken drumsticks, thin steaks and hamburgers — a really thick T-bone steak will dry out too much on one of these. Chargrill pans are commonly made of cast iron, some of which are coated with enamel or anodised aluminium; some also have a non-stick surface. Uncoated cast-iron models require 'curing' before use.

Casserole dishes

Sometimes called Dutch ovens, casserole dishes are designed for moist cooking methods (braising, stewing, pot-roasting) and should be made of a material that keeps and diffuses heat well, such as earthenware, copper, glass, cast iron, stainless steel or aluminium. A good casserole dish will have a thick, heavy base. For maximum versatility, choose one that is quite large so you can pot-roast a whole chicken or large topside if need be. Remember it's always worth braising more meat than you think you'll need — for little extra effort, you'll have tasty leftovers for a few days, or some extra meals

to tuck away in the freezer. The 'classic' casserole dish is deep, round or oval, and made of flameproof enamelled cast iron so it can be used on the stove to brown meat and vegetables and bring a braise to a simmer, then sealed with its heavy, tight-fitting lid and transferred to the oven to finish cooking. Glass, ceramic or stoneware casserole dishes can't be used in this way as they crack over direct heat. A tight-fitting lid is essential to stop liquid evaporating while the meat is braising. The dish should also have good, practical handles, although these aren't usually heat-resistant.

Stockpots

Stockpots are large, tall and narrow to discourage liquid evaporating too quickly while a stock is cooking. Their height also forces heat to bubble up through the ingredients during cooking, helping flavours to disperse and develop, making for a rich and full-flavoured stock. Stockpots are large because it isn't really worth making stock in small amounts. Stockpots can also be used to make soup, boil lobsters and crabs or poach large pieces of meat. Stockpots come in a range of sizes, but choose a large one — it is far more convenient to reduce and freeze excess stock than constantly make it in smaller quantities. Make sure the stockpot has a heavy base for good heat distribution, and so it will hold the stock at a bare simmer. Stainless-steel stockpots are best as they are relatively light (an important consideration as full stockpots are very heavy), but also strong and non-reactive, so they won't discolour or taint if you use acidic ingredients such as tomatoes. It is possible to buy a stockpot with a spigot (tap) fitted near the base, which makes extracting the stock an easy operation. Buy the best-quality stockpot you can possibly afford — it will last you a lifetime and beyond.

Frying pans

These versatile pans can be used for more than just frying — you can sauté in them and also build a sauce from the pan juices after you've finished frying. The best frying pans are those that heat quickly and hold their heat well. For this reason, many cooks prefer cast-iron pans, although copper and stainless-steel pans are better for cooking delicate dishes as cast-iron can impart a metallic taint. Copper and stainless steel also cool down more quickly than cast iron, an advantage when cooking delicate sauces and meats. Carbon-steel pans distribute heat very quickly and evenly, but cheaper ones can warp over high heat. Carbon-steel and cast-iron pans can rust, so they need to be thoroughly washed and dried after use. Non-stick frying pans are very popular, but the non-stick surface does dampen heat transmission somewhat, so choose one with a heavy base that can withstand high direct heat. Also, metal cooking utensils can damage their surface. It's important to find a pan that feels good and balanced to you. Handle design, the height and degree of flare of the sides, the thickness of the base, overall weight and ease of handling are all factors to consider.

TECHNIQUES

BRAISING, POT-ROASTING AND STEWING

These are long, slow, moist methods of cooking, best suited to tougher cuts of meat, which are rich in muscle fibres and connective tissue. It can take several hours for such cuts to reach fall-apart tenderness, but you'll be rewarded with an unctuously full, deliciously complex dish. Braising and stewing are two very similar techniques and easy to master.

Large, whole cuts of meat (a whole beef topside or large piece of brisket) are generally treated as pot roasts, which are technically braises. Pot roasts are generally trimmed of excess fat and tied with kitchen string for a neat shape. The meat is browned all over, then placed in a snug-fitting saucepan with aromatics and a little cooking liquid, then cooked very gently for several hours. Never boil pot roasts or the meat will be tough and stringy.

Braising generally implies large pieces of meat that are cooked, always tightly covered, in some gently simmering liquid until very tender. It is vital that the lid fits tightly to prevent the liquid evaporating; the less liquid used, the more concentrated the flavours will be.

Stewing generally involves smaller pieces of meat that are slowly cooked in sufficient liquid to completely immerse; the pan can be either covered or uncovered and is usually placed on the stovetop, but can also be placed in the oven. The principles and techniques are almost identical to braising.

Usually the meat is browned all over in hot oil or butter before braising, pot-roasting or stewing (two exceptions are the Moroccan tagines and French blanquettes); this helps seal in juices and creates a deeper flavour and colour. Use a heavy-based (preferably cast-iron) casserole dish with a snugly fitting lid for best results with braises and pot roasts; stews are often cooked uncovered as they generally contain more liquid and this helps the liquid evaporate, giving the sauce thickness and body. Often the meat is generously dusted with flour before browning to add body to the finished sauce. Aromatics (herbs, spices, garlic) and vegetables are typically then added, with stock or some other cooking liquid (wine, beer, cider, tomato purée or even orange juice). It is vital that the liquid be kept at a bare simmer to keep the juices in the meat. Very slow cooking is necessary to loosen, soften and ultimately break down connective tissues, and to allow the gelatine in the tissues to give substance to the sauce — none of this can be achieved quickly.

Braises, pot roasts and stews are dishes to make in ample quantity — there's no point cooking them just for two. Leftovers will taste even better after a night maturing in the refrigerator.

Pan-frying

Pan-frying is a relatively fast, high-heat method of cooking where thinner cuts of meat (or patties) are cooked in a pan on the stove in a little oil. (Choose an oil with a high burning point, such as peanut, safflower, soya bean or grapeseed oil — avoid butter and olive, corn or sunflower oils as they will burn.) Medium–thick steaks, thin escalopes or 'minute' steaks, hamburgers, sausages and meatballs are all suited to this treatment.

Choose a frying pan that is large enough to fit all the meat in a single layer without crowding (which can cause the meat to stew), but not so large that the juices in the gaps will spread thinly, evaporate and burn. The pan should have a reasonably heavy base so it doesn't buckle over high heat and will hold its heat well when you introduce the meat: a cast-iron pan is definitely best.

Get your pan quite hot before adding the oil, and have your meat at room temperature to speed up the cooking process. Sear the meat quickly in the very hot pan (it should give a hearty sizzle upon contact) on each side to seal in juices and form a crust, then cook over a slightly reduced heat, turning the meat only once until done to your liking. Meat becomes tougher the more 'done' it is, so it is better to slightly undercook than overcook it — you can always put a slightly underdone piece back in the pan to cook a little longer, but meat that is overdone has lost its tenderness for good.

Poaching

Most poached meat dishes sprang from peasant cooking, where bony pieces of meat were simmered in water with a few aromatics and vegetables — whatever was to hand — to form a humble repast. These days we can use more extravagant ingredients and enjoy such dishes for their own sake. In general, the meat cuts most suitable for poaching are the same as for braising — namely, the hard-working muscles that have loads of connective tissue and gelatine which soften only with long, moist simmering. See the introduction to each meat chapter for specific cuts suitable for poaching.

To poach meat, trim it of excess fat, if necessary, and tie at regular intervals with kitchen string if needed to keep the shape neat. Add the meat to barely simmering water or stock. Meat cooked on the bone is always tastier and this is never truer than with poaching — for extra flavour and body, add a cut of meat from the feet or lower legs (a beef knuckle, cut marrow bones, lamb shanks, pork hocks, calf feet) to the poaching liquid if desired.

During poaching, carefully skim off all the scum or the liquid will become cloudy. Vegetables to be served with the poached meat (as distinct from those used to flavour the stock, which are discarded before serving) are added at an appropriate time so they are tender when the meat is also tender. Use a meat thermometer to test for well done (see the temperature guides in the individual chapter introductions). Once the meat is done, the cooking liquid should be skimmed of all fat and passed through a sieve lined with muslin (cheesecloth) to remove impurities. The stock can be served as a soup to accompany the meat and vegetables (although not from corned beef as it will be too salty), or reduced and ladled over the meat.

Roasting

Little can compare with the crusty, meaty savour of a roasting joint of meat. It has to be good meat for roasting: when meat is cooked this simply, its flavours and textures are fully revealed for what they are — or are not.

Roasting simply involves cooking a large, uncovered cut of meat in quite a hot oven. Typically it is browned first to lock in juices and form a lovely crust. Before cooking, have your meat at room temperature, and your oven fully preheated. Some cuts, such as beef tenderloin (eye fillet), need to be tied with kitchen string to keep their shape. Use a roasting tin that suits the size of your roast — not so large that valuable juices will flow out and burn, or so small it will stew in its own juices. A roast needs to have air flowing around it to cook properly, so many cooks place their roast on a rack inside the roasting tin, although this isn't entirely necessary. Meat roasted on the bone will take a little longer to cook than meat roasted off the bone — a meat thermometer (see page 12) will help you judge how cooked a roast is.

An absolutely vital part of roasting is the resting — the muscle fibres inside the hot meat need time to relax, allowing the juices to settle. If you slice a roast straight out of the oven you will lose much of the juices and your roast will be the lesser for it. Rest your roast at warm room temperature (on top of the stove is ideal) covered loosely with foil. A roast will continue to cook a little as it rests, so allow for this in your cooking-time calculations. Carve the rested roast against the grain using an extremely sharp knife, resisting any temptation to stick a carving fork into the meat (rather, hold the fork upright against the joint to steady it) or you'll lose precious juices.

beef

'Beef,' declared the famous early nineteenth-century French chef Marie-Antoine Carême, 'is the soul of cooking.' In whatever form — a crusty, grill-blackened steak; juicy slices from a perfectly medium–rare roast, doused in meaty gravy; or delicious fried patties in a home-made hamburger — beef is, for many, the 'ultimate' meat.

Beef cattle are believed to have been domesticated about 8000 years ago in the area that is now Turkey. Beef is widely consumed throughout much of the world today, with hundreds of breeds and cross-breeds farmed for this purpose. The top beef-producing countries are the United States, European Union, Brazil, Japan and China, while the top consumers are the Argentineans, whose beef intake is a robust 65 kg (143 lb) per person per year. This compares with about 44 kg (97 lb) per capita in the United States, 38 kg (84 lb) in Australia, 20 kg (44 lb) in Europe and less than 10 kg (22 lb) in Asia.

Until quite recently, cattle were valuable draft animals, essential for pulling wagons and ploughs. Most rural folk couldn't afford to have cows standing around filling up on grass, and they were worked hard. This made for somewhat stringy, chewy meat when they were finally slaughtered. The large beasts also had to be used fairly quickly (or preserved in brine or salt) or the meat, in those days before refrigeration, would spoil. These factors, as well as the cookery technology of the day, hugely influenced the way beef was cooked — it was not unusual throughout Europe for whole cattle to be slowly spit-roasted, then consumed in large chunks. Medieval beef recipes seem strange to us today; throughout Europe it was common for them to be heavily seasoned with strong aromatics (such as mace, ginger, cardamom, saffron and allspice), dried fruits, verjuice and honey. Meat (and spices) were very expensive and generally consumed only by the aristocracy.

Today we have the luxury of being able to buy and store smaller pieces of meat. We also have greater access to alternative cooking traditions — from Argentinean *asado* (barbecue) dishes to Italian carpaccio and Thai beef salads. Unfortunately, many shoppers are stuck on demanding beef that's tender and lean. While many cuts of beef display both of these admirable qualities, it is often the 'lesser' cuts (those that aren't super tender or lean) that are the most interesting and flavoursome when cooked appropriately.

To get the most out of cooking beef, you need to understand where the various cuts come from and what they are good for. It is also vital to know the qualities that identify best-quality fresh beef, and the questions to ask retailers to make sure you're buying it. The difference will be apparent where it matters the most — at the dinner table.

How beef is produced

'Beef' is the meat from full-grown cattle (usually steers, or castrated males) that are about two years old. There are about 50 main breeds of beef cattle, although Angus, Hereford, Shorthorn, Brahman and Charolais are among the best known. The Japanese Wagyu breed produces the revered wagyu or Kobe beef, considered the 'caviar of beef'. Special attention to the care and diet of these cattle produces meat that is intensely marbled with fat (much of it monounsaturated, and so soft it melts at room temperature). Bred for the quality of its yield rather than quantity, wagyu meat is very expensive.

Historically, beef was raised exclusively on pasture, and until the Second World War, all the world's beef was 'grass fed'. Cows are ruminants and their natural diet is forage. In Western agriculture, where efficiency and economics are paramount, all beef cows still spend part of their life on pasture, but many are then moved into higher-density living situations and grain-fed, or 'lot' fed — commonly with corn, barley, soy beans and sorghum to fatten them quickly before slaughter.

Grass-fed beef can cost up to twice as much as grain-fed because the cattle take much longer to mature (about 30 months, compared to 18 for grain-fed) as pasture is much less energy-dense than grain. Lot-fed, or grain-fed, beef has a consistent, uniform flavour and texture that consumers have come to expect, whereas grass-fed cattle can vary greatly in flavour and tenderness, depending on their particular pasture, breed and even climate.

Because grain-fed cattle aren't roaming over (often steep) pasture all day, and are consuming high-kilojoule fodder, they have a lot of fat marbled through their flesh, making for juicy eating. (Good marbling can be achieved in grass-fed beef, but takes considerable management and time.) Grass-fed beef is far leaner than grain-fed, but higher in omega-3 fatty acids, vitamins A and E, and conjugated linoleic acid. The diet of many grain-eating cows also contains additives such as antibiotics (to prevent sickness) and hormones (to encourage growth). 'Mad cow disease' was the result of putting animal-derived waste into cattle feed — routine practice at the time.

Hanging, aging and packaging

Until about 30 years ago, beef was commonly dry-aged before it was sold. Dry-aging involves hanging beef, either as half-carcasses or large chunks, in a humidity-controlled near-freezing cool room for 10–14 days, or even up to 28 days. During this time, natural enzymes in the meat break down connective tissues and fibres, making the flesh more tender. Significant moisture loss also occurs, resulting in deeper, more concentrated, slightly tangy beef flavours and a denser meat (which also cooks more quickly). Only the best grades of beef are dry-aged as the process is expensive, requiring time and space. Consequently it is no longer mainstream practice, although if you ask among your local butchers, you may find a caring retailer who still hangs their beef, most likely for high-end restaurateurs.

In the West, most meat is now vacuum-packed within 24 hours of slaughter and sold within 4 days. If the meat is aged at all, for convenience it is most likely 'wet-aged' (in cryovac packs) at a cool temperature for 7–28 days. The same enzymes are still breaking down the same proteins, but because it occurs in a sealed, wet environment, the meat stays very juicy — although it doesn't have the depth of flavour as dry-aged meat and some say it can taste 'bloody' or 'metallic'. With wet-aged meat, take care that there is no excess blood in the packaging, as the meat may develop 'off' flavours.

Nutritional content

Some people avoid eating beef, worried about fat and cholesterol. However, over recent decades, the meat industry has been developing leaner meats, and not all the fat contained in beef is necessarily 'bad'. Half the fatty acids in beef are monounsaturated (like those in olive oil). A third of the saturated fat is stearic acid, which studies show has a neutral impact on cholesterol.

Beef is a prime source of protein, iron, zinc and vitamin B12. An 85 g (3 oz) serving of beef contains fewer than 10% of the kilojoules needed for the average daily diet, but the same amount of iron as 3 cups of raw spinach, and supplies 39% of our daily zinc requirement, 37% of our daily vitamin B12 requirement and 31% of our daily selenium needs.

Beef is also high in choline, a substance important for memory function and cognition, and contains conjugated linoleic acid (CLA), which has been found to boost immunity, contain cancer-inhibiting properties, and may help prevent diabetes and lower blood cholesterol. Interestingly, grass-fed beef is especially high in CLA.

Buying and storing beef

Do buy beef from a specialist butcher. Look for beef that is deep red and slightly moist, with a smooth grain. It should smell sweet and fresh. Visible fat can vary in colour — that of grain-fed cattle tends to be creamy-white, and grass-fed cattle darker. Avoid meat with very yellowish fat as the meat is well past its prime. Do not buy meat that is very dark purple, brownish, splotchy or very wet, or has a sticky surface or unpleasant smell. Take care not to confuse 'old' meat with 'aged' meat — they are very different things.

Fresh beef can be refrigerated for up to 4 days, but use mince (ground beef) within 2 days. Make sure the beef is dry and not sitting in blood — place larger cuts on a rack above a tray or plate to avoid this. Store meat in the coldest part of the refrigerator. If it is vacuum packed, leave it in its original wrapping. If it isn't, and you intend to refrigerate it for more than a day, remove the plastic and loosely rewrap (so air can flow around it) in fresh plastic wrap or foil. Don't refrigerate larger cuts of meat for longer than 5 days or the meat will turn brown and start to decay.

Vacuum-packed meat will keep, in its original packaging, in the coolest part of the fridge for up to 2 weeks. Store it fat side up to stop it discolouring. When opened, the meat will give off an odour, but this should dissipate after a few minutes. The meat will also change from dark burgundy to bright red upon contact with the air.

Beef can also be frozen for some time; the larger the cut, the longer it will keep. Mince (ground beef) can be frozen for 2–3 months, and larger pieces for 6 months or even up to 9 months. Make sure it is airtight (to avoid 'freezer burn') and very well wrapped to stop it drying out.

Cuts of beef

In a nutshell, there are two types of beef: tender and tough. Think of meat as muscle and you'll soon appreciate why. Muscles that work harder (those in the legs and neck) make for chewier meat, full of connective tissue, gristle and collagen, while those along the back are soft and tender. Basically, beef becomes more tender the further it is from the hoof and horn. It is vital to know what cut you are buying in order to cook it correctly. Some cuts are forever destined for the braising pan or stewing pot, while others only need the briefest of searing over high heat to be rendered delicious.

Beef cuts and names vary between countries (and sometimes even between retailers), but general rules of cookery do apply to any cut from a given area of a carcass, no matter where you live and cook!

Think of a beast in term of four quarters: two big front pieces and two rear pieces. The forequarter sections yield cuts such as boneless shin (or gravy beef), bone-in shin (also wrongly called osso bucco; osso bucco comes from veal), cross rib roast (shoulder clod), brisket, the various cuts of chuck and blade (steak and roast), and the neck and clod (often sold as 'stewing steak' or minced/ground meat). Short ribs (both English-style and flanken-style) can also be cut from this section. The rear part of the forequarter yields fore rib and back rib roasts, and cuts that are called cube roll (scotch fillet) and standing rib roast (and rib cutlets) in some parts of the world; with the exception of these cuts, the meat from this area is best suited for slow, moist methods of cookery such as braising, stewing and pot-roasting.

The hindquarters yield a wide variety of cuts, including the most tender. Sirloin (New York cut), tenderloin (eye fillet), rump (both roast and steaks), topside (roast and steaks) and silverside come from here, as do skirt steak, the flank cuts, oxtail, and the odd tough but tasty cut often just sold as 'braising' steak. Round steak from the knuckle region and bone-in shin meat also comes from the hindquarters.

COOKING BEEF

Braising and stewing

These long, slow, moist methods of cooking suit tougher cuts of meat, which are rich in muscle fibres and connective tissue. Large, whole cuts of beef (a whole topside for example, or large piece of brisket) are generally treated as pot roasts (see page 17), which are also technically braises.

The best cuts for braising and stewing are the shin (both on and off the bone; also called gravy beef), chuck, blade (on or off the bone), neck cuts, spare ribs, tail and skirt steak. Topside and silverside are good braised when cut into steaks or chunks or, when cooked whole, pot-roasted. A whole chuck, skirt or bolar blade can also be pot-roasted.

Pan-frying

This method is good for medium–thick steaks, thin, flat escalopes or 'minute' steaks, hamburgers, beef sausages and meatballs.

Sear the meat quickly in a very hot pan (it should give a hearty sizzle on contact) on each side to seal in juices and form a crust, then cook over a slightly reduced heat, turning the meat *only once,* until done to your liking. If the steak or patty is thickish, you can test doneness using a meat thermometer. Rare beef has an internal temperature of 60°C (140°F), medium 70°C (158°F) and well done 75°C (165°F). Remember that meat becomes tougher and less springy the more 'done' it is, and it is always better to slightly undercook than overcook beef — once it's cooked through, there's no going back.

Cuts suitable for pan-frying include slices of tenderloin (eye fillet), thinnish slices of rump steak, sirloin (New York cut), rib steak, scotch fillet, oyster blade — and with care, decent-sized pieces of porterhouse and T-bone (the pan must not be too searingly hot or the outside will burn before the meat is cooked). Various minced (ground) meat preparations such as hamburgers, meatballs and sausages are also ideal.

Poaching

Many famous so-called 'boiled' beef dishes aren't boiled at all, but are in fact simmered gently or poached. The Spanish have their *cocido madrileno*, the Americans their New England boiled dinner, and the English their beloved corned beef (which comes from the days when meat was preserved in salted brine, and which is still enjoyed today for its flavour and texture).

Beef cuts most suitable for poaching are the same as for braising — namely, the hard-working muscles that have loads of connective tissue and gelatine which soften only with long, moist simmering. A notable exception is tenderloin (eye fillet), which as the French know is wonderful poached — it is the meat used in *boeuf à la ficelle* (see page 38). Use a meat thermometer to test for well done (see temperature guide above) — although poached beef fillet should only be cooked to medium.

The best cuts for poaching are brisket, corned beef, shank, bottom round (braising steak) and tenderloin.

Roasting

This simple method of cooking beef to mouth-watering perfection deserves only the best-quality meat. A very small roast is best browned in a large pan on the stove; a larger roast can be roasted in a very hot oven (240°C/475°F/Gas 8) for about 20 minutes, or a very large roast for up to 35–40 minutes, to seal the meat. The heat is then reduced to 180°C (350°F/Gas 4) and the meat roasted until done. As a general guide, after the initial browning, roast meat for 15 minutes per 500 g (1 lb 2 oz) for rare, 20 minutes for medium, and 25 minutes for well done — but remember roasted beef really is best when juicily pink and medium–rare. A meat thermometer is a convenient way to judge how cooked a roast is.

The exception to the above cooking guide is beef tenderloin (fillet), which is so lean and tender that it should be cooked as quickly as possible so it doesn't dry out. Roast it at 240°C (475°F/Gas 8) for 7 minutes per 500 g (1 lb 2 oz) for rare, and 10 minutes for medium.

Once cooked, rest your roast for 20 minutes (but longer for a very large joint) at warm room temperature, covered loosely with foil — on top of the stove is ideal. A roast will continue to cook a little as it rests, so allow for this in your cooking calculations.

The best cuts for roasting are rib roasts (standing rib, boneless rolled rib, rib-eye fillet — also called cube roll), whole beef tenderloin (eye fillet), a whole sirloin (top loin or New York strip) or rump, and, if you can get it, the tri-tip or triangle roast, which is sometimes cut from the sirloin.

Slow roasting is better for lean or not so tender cuts such as topside or whole bolar blade, which are not suitable to be cooked very pink. The browning procedure is omitted, and often a very lean joint will be covered with a thin layer of added fat (such as overlapping slices of fatty bacon) to stop it drying out. The meat is then gently roasted at 150°C (300°F/Gas 2) — or as low as 130°C (250°F/Gas 1) — until evenly cooked through, then rested. As a rough guide, slow-roasted beef needs 20–25 minutes per 500 g (1 lb 2 oz) for medium and 30–35 minutes for well done.

Good cuts for slow roasting are silverside, topside, whole bolar blade, whole skirt, rump roast, bottom round roast (USA) and eye of round (USA).

Minced beef

Commercially minced (ground) meat is of dubious provenance and usually too finely minced to be an interesting ingredient. Grinding breaks down the connective tissues and fibres in cheaper, tougher cuts of beef, but in the process moisture is lost. Mince is sold in various grades, with the highest and leanest being topside mince; lower grades contain 25–30% fat. Leanest isn't necessarily 'best', as some dishes (such as pasta sauces) require some fat for lubrication; others, such as hamburgers, are better with a coarser texture.

You can easily mince your own beef using a mincing attachment on an electric mixer, a hand-cranked mincer, or the truly old-fashioned way — using two large, sharp knives. Mince tougher, stewing cuts for long-cooked mince dishes such as lasagne, bolognaise and chilli bowl, and use topside mince for meatballs, meatloaves and hamburgers. For steak tartare, which is based on raw minced beef tenderloin (eye fillet), rump or sirloin, the meat should always be chopped by hand.

Souvlaki with fennel salad

Serves 4

1 kg (2 lb 4 oz) beef rump or sirloin, trimmed and cut into 2 cm (3/4 inch) pieces
3 tablespoons olive oil
2 teaspoons finely grated lemon zest
4 tablespoons lemon juice
125 ml (4 fl oz/1/2 cup) dry white wine
2 teaspoons dried oregano
2 large garlic cloves, finely chopped
2 bay leaves
crusty bread, to serve

GARLIC YOGHURT SAUCE
250 g (9 oz/1 cup) Greek-style yoghurt
2 garlic cloves, crushed

FENNEL SALAD
2 large fennel bulbs
1 tablespoon lemon juice
1 tablespoon extra virgin olive oil
2 teaspoons red wine vinegar
150 g (5 1/2 oz/1 cup) pitted niçoise olives

Put the beef in a non-metallic bowl with 2 tablespoons of the olive oil, the lemon zest, lemon juice, wine, oregano, garlic, bay leaves and some freshly ground black pepper. Toss to combine well, then cover and refrigerate overnight.

About half an hour before you are ready to cook, mix together the garlic yoghurt sauce ingredients and set aside.

Start preparing the fennel salad. Trim the fennel bulbs, reserving the fronds, and discard the tough outer layers. Using a very sharp knife, very thinly slice the fennel lengthways and place in a bowl of very cold water with the lemon juice. Set aside until nearly ready to serve.

Preheat a barbecue chargrill plate to medium–high. Drain the beef and thread onto eight metal skewers. Cook for 5–7 minutes for medium–rare, or until done to your liking, brushing the beef with the remaining olive oil and turning often during cooking.

Meanwhile, drain the fennel well, pat dry with paper towels and toss in a serving bowl with the olive oil and vinegar. Finely chop the fennel fronds, add them to the fennel with the olives and season to taste with freshly ground black pepper.

Serve the souvlaki with the garlic yoghurt sauce, fennel salad and crusty bread.

Parmesan carpaccio

Serves 2–4

400 g (14 oz) piece of fillet steak, trimmed (see Note)
2 tablespoons lemon juice
3 tablespoons virgin olive oil
1 hard-boiled egg
½ celery stalk, cut into julienne strips
50 g (1¾ oz/½ cup) shaved parmesan cheese
baby rocket (arugula) leaves, to garnish (optional)

Freeze the beef for about 2 hours, or until firm but not frozen solid. Using a large, sharp knife, cut it into very thin slices.

Lay the beef slices, slightly overlapping, on serving plates. Sprinkle with the lemon juice, olive oil and some sea salt and freshly ground black pepper. Push the yolk of the egg through a regular sieve (reserve the white for another use). Sprinkle the egg yolk over the beef, then scatter with the celery and parmesan. Serve immediately, garnished with rocket leaves if desired.

NOTE: Make sure the meat is very fresh and of the highest quality.

MARINATED BEEF RIBS IN DARK ALE AND MUSTARD

SERVES 4

4 beef spare ribs (about 2 kg/4 lb 8 oz in total), cut in half (ask your butcher to do this)
125 ml (4 fl oz/½ cup) dark ale
2 tablespoons soft brown sugar
3 tablespoons cider vinegar
2 small red chillies, seeded and finely chopped
2 tablespoons ground cumin
1 tablespoon wholegrain mustard
20 g (¾ oz) unsalted butter

Place the ribs in a single layer in a large non-metallic dish. Put the ale, sugar, vinegar, chilli, cumin and mustard in a bowl, stir well to dissolve the sugar, then pour over the ribs. Toss to coat, then cover and marinate in the refrigerator for 1–2 hours.

Preheat a kettle or covered barbecue to medium indirect heat. Transfer the ribs and the marinade to a large shallow roasting tin and place in the middle of the barbecue. Lower the lid and cook the ribs for 50 minutes, or until the meat is tender and about 125 ml (4 fl oz/½ cup) of marinade is left in the roasting tin. Transfer the ribs to a warm serving plate while you finish making the sauce — leave the roasting tin on the barbecue to keep warm.

Using a whisk, beat the butter into the reduced marinade in the roasting tin and season with sea salt and freshly ground black pepper.

Divide the ribs among four warmed plates and serve drizzled with the sauce.

Beef fillet cooked in red wine

Serves 4

- 750 g (1 lb 10 oz) trimmed beef fillet, cut from the thick end of the fillet
- 3 garlic cloves, thinly sliced
- 2 tablespoons chopped rosemary
- 8–10 thin slices of prosciutto, pancetta or smoked bacon
- 20 g (3/4 oz) dried wild mushrooms, such as porcini
- 2 tablespoons olive oil
- 1 onion, cut in half, then sliced
- 150 ml (5 fl oz) full-bodied red wine, such as Barolo, cabernet sauvignon or shiraz
- 400 g (14 oz) tin chopped tomatoes

Using a small, sharp knife, make several small incisions in the beef. Push a slice of garlic into each incision and reserve the remaining garlic slices. Scatter half the rosemary over the beef and season with sea salt and freshly ground black pepper. Overlap the prosciutto slices on a board to create a 'sheet' of prosciutto to wrap the beef in. Lay the beef across the prosciutto sheet, then carefully wrap the prosciutto around the beef to completely enclose the fillet. Using kitchen string, tie the fillet at 5 cm (2 inch) intervals, then place in the refrigerator to rest for 15 minutes.

Preheat the oven to 190°C (375°F/Gas 5). Soak the mushrooms in 200 ml (7 fl oz) hot water for 10 minutes and set aside.

Heat the olive oil in a large flameproof casserole dish. Add the beef and cook over high heat, turning often, until the prosciutto is golden brown all over (it doesn't matter if some prosciutto falls off). Remove the beef from the casserole dish.

Add the onion to the casserole dish and sauté over medium heat for 6–7 minutes, or until soft. Add the remaining garlic and rosemary and cook for a few minutes until fragrant.

Drain the mushrooms well, reserving the soaking water. Add the mushrooms to the onion mixture and cook for a further 2 minutes. Add the mushroom liquid, discarding any sediment, then boil until the liquid is very reduced. Stir in the wine and cook for 2–3 minutes, then add the tomatoes and cook for a further 5–10 minutes, or until thickened into a sauce. Season with sea salt and freshly ground black pepper.

Add the beef, turning to coat in the sauce. Cover and bake for 15 minutes for rare, or 20 minutes for medium–rare. Remove from the oven, cover loosely with foil and leave to rest in a warm place for at least 15 minutes.

Remove the beef from the sauce and remove the string. Carve the beef into 2 cm (3/4 inch) slices. Divide among warmed plates, spoon the sauce over and serve.

Tagliatelle with ragù

Serves 4

60 g ($2^{1}/_{4}$ oz) butter
1 onion, finely chopped
1 celery stalk, finely chopped
1 carrot, finely chopped
90 g ($3^{1}/_{4}$ oz) pancetta or bacon, finely chopped
225 g (8 oz) minced (ground) beef
225 g (8 oz) minced (ground) pork
2 oregano sprigs, chopped, or $^{1}/_{4}$ teaspoon dried oregano
a pinch of nutmeg
125 g ($4^{1}/_{2}$ oz) chicken livers, trimmed (see page 153) and finely chopped
125 ml (4 fl oz/$^{1}/_{2}$ cup) dry white wine
185 ml (6 fl oz/$^{3}/_{4}$ cup) milk
400 g (14 oz) tin chopped tomatoes
250 ml (9 fl oz/1 cup) beef stock
400 g (14 oz) dried tagliatelle, or 500 g (1 lb 2 oz) fresh pasta
grated parmesan cheese, to serve

Heat the butter in a saucepan. Add the onion, celery, carrot and pancetta and cook over medium heat, stirring from time to time, for 6–8 minutes, or until the vegetables have softened.

Add the beef, pork, oregano and nutmeg and season with sea salt and freshly ground black pepper. Cook, stirring to break up any lumps, for 5 minutes, or until the meat has changed colour but is not browned. Add the chicken liver and cook until it changes colour.

Add the wine, increase the heat to high and boil for 2–3 minutes, or until the wine has almost completely evaporated. Stir in 125 ml (4 lf oz/$^{1}/_{2}$ cup) of the milk, reduce the heat and simmer for 10 minutes.

Stir in the tomatoes and half the stock. Partially cover and simmer over very low heat for 3 hours, stirring occasionally, and adding more stock as needed to keep the sauce moist.

Cook the pasta in a large saucepan of boiling salted water until *al dente*. Stir the remaining milk into the sauce 5 minutes before serving and season to taste. Drain the pasta, toss with the sauce and serve sprinkled with parmesan.

Beef and beet borscht

Serves 4

2 tablespoons olive oil
1 onion, chopped
2 garlic cloves, crushed
500 g (1 lb 2 oz) beef chuck steak, cut into 2 cm (¾ inch) chunks
1 litre (35 fl oz/4 cups) beef stock
2 small beetroot (beets), scrubbed and trimmed
200 g (7 oz) tinned chopped tomatoes
1 carrot, cut into 1 cm (½ inch) cubes
2 potatoes, peeled and cut into 1 cm (½ inch) cubes
190 g (6¾ oz/2½ cups) finely shredded cabbage
2 teaspoons lemon juice
2 teaspoons sugar
2 tablespoons chopped flat-leaf (Italian) parsley
2 tablespoons chopped dill
4 tablespoons sour cream
crusty bread, to serve

Preheat the oven to 200°C (400°F/Gas 6). Heat the olive oil in a large saucepan, add the onion and garlic and sauté over medium heat for 5 minutes. Add the beef, stock and 1 litre (35 fl oz/4 cups) water and bring to the boil. Reduce the heat and simmer, covered, for 1¼ hours, or until the meat is tender. Remove the meat, reserving the stock mixture.

Meanwhile, wrap each beetroot in foil and bake for 30–40 minutes, or until tender. Remove the foil and leave to cool, then peel and cut into 1 cm (½ inch) pieces (wear gloves to stop your hands staining).

Return the stock to the boil. Add the tomato, carrot and potato and season with sea salt. Cook over medium heat for 10 minutes, or until the vegetables are tender. Add the cabbage and cook for 5 minutes.

Return the meat to the pan with the beetroot, lemon juice, sugar and 1½ tablespoons each of the parsley and dill. Cook for 2 minutes, or until heated through. Season to taste.

Divide the borscht among warmed bowls. Top each with a spoonful of sour cream, sprinkle with the remaining chopped herbs and serve with crusty bread.

Rib eye of beef with spice rub, merlot reduction and orange sweet potato mash

Serves 4

SPICE RUB

1 tablespoon olive oil
1 tablespoon ground coriander
2 teaspoons ground cumin
2 teaspoons smoked paprika
2 teaspoons soft brown sugar
1 teaspoon garlic powder
1 teaspoon salt
½ teaspoon ground black pepper

4 x 280 g (10 oz) rib eye of beef, bone in (beef cutlets from a rack)
450 g (1 lb) orange sweet potato, peeled and chopped
50 g (1¾ oz) butter
3 tablespoons thick (double/heavy) cream
1 tablespoon olive oil

MERLOT REDUCTION

250 ml (9 fl oz/1 cup) beef stock
250 ml (9 fl oz/1 cup) merlot
1 teaspoon caster (superfine) sugar

Mix the spice rub ingredients together and rub well into both sides of each steak. Cover and leave to rest for 30 minutes.

To make the merlot reduction, combine the stock, merlot and sugar in a small saucepan. Bring to the boil, then reduce the heat to medium and cook until the liquid has reduced by one-third. Season to taste with sea salt and freshly ground black pepper.

To make the sweet potato mash, put the sweet potato in a saucepan, cover with water and bring to the boil. Cook for 15 minutes, or until tender. Drain well, then place in a food processor with the butter, cream and a little sea salt and freshly ground black pepper. Purée until smooth and creamy.

Heat a barbecue grill plate or chargrill pan to medium–high. Brush with the olive oil, then add the steaks and cook for 4 minutes on each side for medium–rare, or until done to your liking. Transfer to a warm plate, cover loosely with foil and leave to rest in a warm place for 5 minutes.

Divide the sweet potato mash among four warmed plates. Add the steaks, ladle the merlot reduction over and serve.

BOEUF À LA FICELLE

SERVES 4

750 g (1 lb 10 oz) piece of centre-cut beef fillet or tenderloin (eye fillet)
875 ml (30 fl oz/3½ cups) beef stock
1 swede (rutabaga), cut into batons
1 carrot, cut into batons
1 celery stalk, cut into batons
2 potatoes, peeled and cut into chunks
¼ cabbage, chopped
4 spring onions (scallions), trimmed and cut into long lengths
1 bay leaf
2 thyme sprigs
a few parsley sprigs

Trim the beef of any fat and sinew and cut into four even pieces. Using kitchen string, tie each piece of beef around its circumference so it keeps its compact shape; leave a length of string attached so you can easily lower the beef into the simmering stock later on.

Pour the stock into a saucepan, bring to the boil and add the vegetables and herbs. Cook over medium heat for 8 minutes, or until the vegetables are tender. Remove the vegetables with a slotted spoon and keep warm. Discard the herbs and skim off any scum from the stock.

Season the beef portions with sea salt, then lower them into the simmering stock, keeping the strings tied around the saucepan handle or around a wooden spoon balanced over the saucepan. Cook over medium–low heat for about 6 minutes for rare, or 10 minutes for medium–rare — take care not to let the stock simmer too vigorously.

Remove the beef from the stock and remove the strings. Divide the beef among warmed, large shallow bowls. Add the cooked vegetables, then ladle some of the cooking liquid over and serve.

Silverside with parsley sauce

Serves 6

1.5 kg (3 lb 5 oz) corned silverside
1 teaspoon black peppercorns
5 cloves
2 bay leaves, torn
2 tablespoons soft brown sugar

PARSLEY SAUCE
50 g (1¾ oz) butter
1½ tablespoons plain (all-purpose) flour
400 ml (14 fl oz) milk
125 ml (4 fl oz/½ cup) beef stock
2 tablespoons chopped parsley

Soak the silverside in cold water for 45 minutes, changing the water three or four times to remove the excess salt.

Drain the silverside, then place in a large heavy-based saucepan with the peppercorns, cloves, bay leaves, sugar and enough cold water to just cover. Bring to the boil, then reduce the heat to very low and simmer for 1½–1¾ hours, turning the beef over every half hour and adding water as needed to keep the beef covered. Take care not to let the water boil as this will toughen the meat. Remove the beef from the liquid and leave to rest in a warm place for 15 minutes.

To make the parsley sauce, melt the butter in a saucepan over medium heat, then add the flour and stir for 1 minute. Remove the pan from the heat and add the milk and stock, whisking until smooth. Return the pan to the heat and cook, whisking constantly, until the sauce boils and thickens. Reduce the heat and simmer for 2 minutes, then add the parsley and sea salt and freshly ground black pepper to taste.

Slice the silverside and divide among warmed plates. Spoon the parsley sauce over and serve. Steamed vegetables are a traditional accompaniment.

Beef, parsnip, prune and prosciutto salad

Serves 6

DRESSING

1 1/2 tablespoons dijon mustard
1 egg yolk
3 tablespoons red wine vinegar
250 ml (9 fl oz/1 cup) olive oil
4 tablespoons torn basil leaves

125 ml (4 fl oz/ 1/2 cup) dry marsala
24 pitted prunes
1 kg (2 lb 4 oz) piece of beef fillet, trimmed
90 ml (3 fl oz) olive oil
600 g (1 lb 5 oz) parsnips, peeled and cut into rounds 5 mm (1/4 inch) thick
2 red onions, peeled and cut into wedges
100 g (3 1/2 oz) thinly sliced prosciutto
1 radicchio, outer leaves discarded, leaves washed, dried and torn into pieces
150 g (5 1/2 oz/1 bunch) rocket (arugula), trimmed, washed and dried

To make the dressing, put the mustard, egg yolk and vinegar in a large bowl and whisk well. Whisking constantly, add the olive oil in a very slow, steady stream — the mixture should emulsify and thicken. Season to taste with sea salt and freshly ground black pepper, then add the basil and stir to combine. If the dressing is too thick (it should have the consistency of thick pouring cream), stir in a little hot water. Set aside.

Bring the marsala to the boil in a small saucepan. Add the prunes, remove from the heat and stir well. Cover and set aside until cool.

Preheat the oven to 220°C (425°F/Gas 7). Using kitchen string, tie the beef at 5 cm (2 inch) intervals to form a neat shape. Heat 2 tablespoons of the olive oil in a large, ovenproof frying pan, add the beef and cook over high heat for 3–4 minutes, turning to brown all over. Season with sea salt and freshly ground black pepper, then transfer the pan to the oven and roast the beef for 17–20 minutes for medium–rare, or until cooked to your liking. Remove from the oven, cover loosely with foil and set aside to rest.

Reduce the oven temperature to 200°C (400°F/Gas 6). Put the parsnip and onion in a large roasting tin, add the remaining olive oil and toss to coat. Roast for 20 minutes, or until golden and tender, turning once. Drain well on paper towels, then leave to cool to room temperature.

Remove the string from the beef. Thinly slice the beef and place in a large bowl with the drained prunes, roasted vegetables, prosciutto, radicchio and rocket and toss well. Divide among six plates, drizzle with the dressing and serve.

Roast beef with red wine sauce and Yorkshire puddings

Serves 8

250 ml (9 fl oz/1 cup) red wine
2 bay leaves
1 onion, finely chopped
4 whole cloves
1 teaspoon cracked black peppercorns
2.5 kg (5 lb 8 oz) boneless beef rib roast
250 ml (9 fl oz/1 cup) home-made beef stock (see Note)
160 g (5½ oz/½ cup) plum jam
1 tablespoon cornflour (cornstarch)

YORKSHIRE PUDDINGS
olive oil, for greasing
250 g (9 oz/2 cups) self-raising flour
2 eggs, lightly beaten
375 ml (13 fl oz/1½ cups) milk

Put the wine, bay leaves, onion, cloves and peppercorns in a large non-metallic dish and stir to combine. Add the beef, turning to coat, then cover and refrigerate for 4 hours or overnight, turning the meat occasionally. Drain the meat well, reserving the marinade.

Preheat the oven to 210°C (415°F/Gas 6–7). Place the meat on a roasting rack in a deep flameproof roasting tin and pour in 170 ml (5½ fl oz/⅔ cup) water. Roast for 1½ hours for rare, 1 hour 40 minutes for medium or 2 hours for well done, basting the meat occasionally with the reserved marinade.

Meanwhile, pour the stock into a saucepan and allow to boil for 15–20 minutes, or until reduced by two-thirds. Set aside.

Remove the roast to a warm platter, reserving the roasting tin, then cover loosely with foil and leave to rest in a warm place. Increase the oven temperature to 240°C (475°F/Gas 8).

While the roast is resting, make the Yorkshire puddings. Prepare two deep, 6-hole muffin tins by pouring a teaspoon of olive oil into each hole. Heat the tins in the oven for 10 minutes, or until the oil is smoking.

Place the flour in a bowl and make a well in the centre. Mix together the eggs and milk, then pour into the well and stir to make a smooth batter. Half-fill each hot muffin hole with the batter, then bake for 15 minutes, or until the puddings are well risen and golden.

While the puddings are baking, pour off the excess fat from the roasting juices in the roasting tin, then place the tin over low heat. Add the reserved marinade and the jam and stir over low heat until the mixture boils. Blend the cornflour with the reduced stock to form a smooth paste, then, stirring constantly, add it to the marinade mixture. Stir over medium heat for 3 minutes, or until the sauce boils and thickens. Strain and set aside, then keep warm over low heat.

Carve the rested roast. Serve the hot puddings straight from the oven with the sliced roast and the warm sauce.

NOTE: It is important to use home-made stock for this recipe as ready-made stock is too salty and won't reduce to the right thickness for the sauce.

Beef pot roast provençal

Serves 6

3 tomatoes
2 tablespoons olive oil
2 kg (4 lb 8 oz) rolled beef brisket, trimmed
750 ml (26 fl oz/3 cups) beef stock
250 ml (9 fl oz/1 cup) red wine
3 tablespoons brandy
2 onions, quartered
3 garlic cloves, crushed
2 bay leaves
a small handful of chopped parsley
2 tablespoons thyme
12 pitted black olives
6 small carrots, thickly sliced
2 tablespoons plain (all-purpose) flour

Using a small, sharp knife, score a small cross in the base of each tomato. Plunge into boiling water for 20 seconds, then drain and plunge into iced water to cool. Peel the skin away from the cross, then cut the tomatoes in half. Scoop out the seeds, chop the flesh and set aside.

Heat the olive oil in a deep, heavy-based saucepan. Add the beef in batches and cook over medium–high heat for 8 minutes, turning to brown all over.

Return all the beef to the pan and add the chopped tomatoes, stock, wine, brandy, onion, garlic, bay leaves, parsley and thyme. Cover and bring to a simmer. Cook over low heat for 1½ hours, then add the olives and carrot and cook for a further 30 minutes.

Remove the beef to a plate, cover loosely with foil and leave to rest in a warm place for 10 minutes.

Put the flour in a small bowl and stir in 3 tablespoons water to form a smooth paste. Add the paste to the saucepan, stir constantly over medium heat until the sauce thickens, then cook for 3 minutes.

Carve the beef and serve drizzled with the sauce.

Boeuf en croûte

Serves 6

PÂTÉ
180 g (6 oz) butter, softened
3 shallots, chopped
1 garlic clove, chopped
360 g (12¾ oz) chicken livers, trimmed (see page 153)
1 tablespoon brandy or Cognac

1 kg (2 lb 4 oz) piece of thick beef fillet, trimmed (see Note)
30 g (1 oz) dripping or clarified butter
600 g (1 lb 5 oz) ready-made puff pastry
1 egg, lightly beaten

To make the pâté, melt half the butter in a frying pan and add the shallot and garlic. Cook over low–medium heat for 7 minutes, or until softened but not browned.

Rinse the chicken livers and pat dry with paper towels. Increase the heat to medium–high and add the livers to the frying pan. Sauté for 4–5 minutes, or until cooked but still a little pink in the middle. Allow to cool completely, then tip the livers and the pan juices into a food processor with the remaining butter and the brandy. Blend until smooth, then season to taste with sea salt and freshly ground black pepper.

Preheat the oven to 220°C (425°F/Gas 7). Using kitchen string, tie the beef at 5 cm (2 inch) intervals to form a neat shape. Heat the dripping in a flameproof roasting tin, add the beef, then sear over medium–high heat for 3–4 minutes, turning to brown all over. Transfer to the oven and roast for 20 minutes, then remove from the oven and allow to cool. Remove the string.

Meanwhile, reduce the oven temperature to 200°C (400°F/Gas 6). Roll the pastry into a rectangle just big enough to enclose the beef fillet completely. Trim the edges and reserve for decoration. Spread the pâté over the pastry, leaving a 1 cm (½ inch) border around the edge. Brush the border with the beaten egg.

Lay the beef fillet on the pastry and wrap it up tightly like a parcel, pressing the seams together firmly and tucking the ends under. Put the parcel, seam side down, on a baking tray and brush all over with the beaten egg. Cut pieces from the pastry trimmings to decorate the pastry, arrange them on top and brush with beaten egg. Bake for 25–30 minutes for rare beef, or 35–40 minutes for medium. Remove from the oven and allow to rest for 5 minutes before carving.

NOTE: For this dish to work really well, ask your butcher for a piece of centre-cut beef fillet that is an even thickness all the way along. This dish is also known as Beef Wellington.

Steak sandwich with roasted red onion sauce

Serves 4

ROASTED RED ONION SAUCE
500 g (1 lb 2 oz) red onions, thinly sliced
1 kg (2 lb 4 oz) baby onions
3 large garlic cloves
2 tablespoons olive oil
1.5 kg (3 lb 5 oz) roma (plum) tomatoes, cut in half lengthways
1 teaspoon sea salt
3 tablespoons chopped oregano
400 g (14 oz) tin chopped tomatoes
1 tablespoon brandy
1 tablespoon soft brown sugar

1 tablespoon olive oil
4 thin sirloin, eye fillet or rump steaks
4 large pieces of ciabatta or pide (Turkish/flat bread), cut in half horizontally
rocket (arugula) leaves, to serve

Preheat the oven to 200°C (400°F/Gas 6). To make the roasted red onion sauce, put the red onion, baby onions, garlic and half the olive oil in a large roasting tin, then toss to coat the onions well. Add the roma tomatoes, drizzle with the remaining oil and sprinkle with the sea salt and oregano. Roast for 1 hour.

Spoon the tinned tomatoes and juice into the roasting tin, taking care not to break up the roasted tomatoes. Drizzle the brandy over the top, sprinkle with the sugar and roast for 20 minutes. Remove from the oven and leave to cool slightly.

When you're ready to eat, heat the olive oil in a frying pan and fry the steaks for 1 minute on each side — they should cook very quickly and start to brown.

While the steaks are cooking, toast the bread. Spread some roasted red onion sauce on half the bread slices, top each with some rocket leaves and a steak, top with the remaining bread and serve.

NOTE: Store any leftover roasted red onion sauce in the fridge to use as a sandwich relish.

Beef 'olives'

Serves 4

STUFFING

125 g (4½ oz/1½ cups) fresh white breadcrumbs
50 g (1¾ oz/½ cup) grated parmesan cheese
3 tablespoons chopped raisins
3 tablespoons pine nuts, toasted and finely chopped
2½ tablespoons capers, finely chopped
a small handful of parsley, chopped
½ teaspoon finely grated lemon zest
a pinch of nutmeg
1 egg, lightly beaten
1 tablespoon dry white wine

4 slices of skirt steak (600 g/1 lb 5 oz in total), cut in half
50 g (1¾ oz) clarified butter
a small handful of basil, roughly chopped

RED WINE SAUCE

1 onion, chopped
2 garlic cloves, crushed
250 ml (9 fl oz/1 cup) beef stock
250 ml (9 fl oz/1 cup) red wine
1 tablespoon plain (all-purpose) flour
20 g (¾ oz) butter

Preheat the oven to 160°C (315°F/Gas 2–3). To make the stuffing, put the breadcrumbs, parmesan, raisins, pine nuts, capers, parsley, lemon zest and nutmeg in a bowl, then add the beaten egg and wine and stir well using a fork. Season to taste with sea salt and freshly ground black pepper.

Lay each piece of steak between two sheets of plastic wrap and pound with a meat pounder to measure about 16 x 14 cm (6¼ x 5½ inches). Divide the stuffing among the steaks, shaping the stuffing into a 'sausage' down the centre of each one, then roll the meat up, tucking in the ends. Tie the rolls with kitchen string to form a neat shape.

Melt the butter in a 2.5 litre (87 fl oz/10 cup) flameproof casserole dish over medium–high heat. Add the beef parcels and cook for 2–3 minutes, turning to brown all over. Remove from the dish and set aside.

To make the red wine sauce, add the onion and garlic to the casserole dish and sauté for 5 minutes, or until the onion has softened. Add the stock and wine and stir for 1–2 minutes. Add the beef parcels to the casserole dish in a single layer, then cover and bake for 1 hour, or until tender.

Remove the beef parcels from the sauce, cut off the strings, then cover loosely with foil and keep warm.

Mix the flour and butter in a bowl to form a paste. Return the casserole dish to the stovetop and bring the sauce to a simmer. Whisking constantly, slowly add the paste. Whisk until the sauce returns to a simmer, then cook, stirring occasionally, for 5 minutes, or until the sauce has thickened. Return the beef parcels to the casserole and reheat gently.

Cut each beef parcel into three or four slices, divide among warmed plates, then drizzle with the red wine sauce and sprinkle with the basil.

Stifado

Serves 6–8

- 4 tablespoons olive oil
- 1.8 kg (4 lb) round or chuck beef, cut into 3 cm (1¼ inch) cubes
- 1 teaspoon ground cumin
- 2 onions, finely chopped
- 3 garlic cloves, crushed
- 250 ml (9 fl oz/1 cup) dry red wine
- 3 tablespoons tomato paste (concentrated purée)
- 4 tablespoons red wine vinegar
- 2 cinnamon sticks
- 10 cloves
- 2 bay leaves
- 2 teaspoons sugar
- 1 kg (2 lb 4 oz) baby onions
- 4 tablespoons currants
- 200 g (7 oz) feta cheese, cut into small cubes
- steamed rice, to serve

Heat half the olive oil in a large flameproof casserole dish. Add the beef in batches and cook over high heat for 3–4 minutes, turning to brown all over, and adding more oil as needed. Put the beef in a bowl, then sprinkle with the cumin and set aside. Add more oil to the dish, add the onion and garlic and sauté over low heat for 5–6 minutes, or until the onion has softened. Return the beef to the casserole.

Add the wine, increase the heat and stir to loosen any bits stuck to the bottom of the dish. Stir in 500 ml (17 fl oz/ 2 cups) water, the tomato paste, vinegar, cinnamon sticks, cloves, bay leaves and sugar. Season with sea salt and freshly ground black pepper and bring to the boil. Reduce the heat to low, cover the casserole dish with a double layer of foil, then the lid. Simmer over low heat for 1 hour.

Peel the onions, cut a small cross into the base, then add to the casserole with the currants. Cook for a further 1 hour, or until the beef is very tender and the sauce is thick. Discard the cinnamon sticks and bay leaves. Stir in the feta and simmer, uncovered, for 3–4 minutes. Serve with steamed rice.

Roast beef with beets and horseradish cream

Serves 6–8

2 large onions
10 thyme sprigs
100 g (3½ oz) butter, softened
3 tablespoons dijon mustard
3–3.5 kg (6 lb 12 oz–7 lb 14 oz) piece of beef forerib on the bone, or a standing rib roast (see Note)
1 tablespoon plain (all-purpose) flour
8 beetroot (beets), scrubbed and trimmed

HORSERADISH CREAM
50 g (1¾ oz/½ cup) peeled fresh horseradish, soaked in cold water for 1 hour
1 teaspoon caster (superfine) sugar
½ teaspoon mustard powder
2 teaspoons white wine vinegar
150 ml (5 fl oz) cream

Preheat the oven to 230°C (450°F/Gas 8). Peel the onions and cut each widthways into six slices. Reserve eight of the smaller slices, then put the rest in the centre of a large roasting tin.

Chop two of the thyme sprigs and place in a small bowl. Add the butter and mustard and mix until smooth, then season with a little salt and plenty of freshly ground black pepper. Wipe the beef well with damp paper towels, then rub all over with half the mustard butter. Place the beef, fat side up, on the onions in the tin. Sprinkle the flour over the beef.

Cut a shallow cross into the top of each beetroot, rest each one on top of a reserved onion ring, then place around the beef. Spoon ¼ teaspoon of the remaining mustard butter on top of each and reserve the rest.

Roast for 20 minutes, then reduce the oven temperature to 160°C (315°F/Gas 2–3) and roast for a further 35 minutes per kilogram (2 lb 4 oz) of beef, basting the beef and beetroot every 30 minutes. Roast for an additional 20 minutes for medium, or 35 minutes for well done.

Turn the oven off. Top each beetroot with ¼ teaspoon of mustard butter and a thyme sprig, then spread the remaining butter over the roast. Return the roast to the oven, leave the door slightly ajar and leave to rest for 15 minutes.

To make the horseradish cream, dry the horseradish thoroughly and grate very finely. Combine in a bowl with the sugar, mustard and vinegar. Whip the cream until it forms soft peaks, then fold into the horseradish mixture and season to taste with sea salt and freshly ground black pepper. Spoon into a serving bowl.

Carve the beef and arrange on a warmed platter. Top with the onion slices, and arrange the beetroot around the edges, cutting them into smaller pieces if desired.

NOTE: Have your butcher 'chine' the joint (cut through the tip of the vertebrae within the joint) to make carving easier; cap the ends of the exposed ribs with foil to stop them burning during cooking.

Beef and spinach salad with orange-mustard dressing

Serves 4

ORANGE-MUSTARD DRESSING
150 g (5½ oz) Greek-style yoghurt
2 teaspoons finely grated orange zest
2½ tablespoons orange juice
3 tablespoons thickened cream
2 garlic cloves, crushed
1 tablespoon wholegrain mustard

200 g (7 oz) green beans, trimmed
100 g (3½ oz/2 cups) baby English spinach leaves
50 g (1¾ oz/1⅔ cups) watercress sprigs
200 g (7 oz) semi-dried (sun-blushed) tomatoes, halved
750 g (1 lb 10 oz) rump steaks, each cut 3 cm (1¼ inches) thick
olive oil, for brushing
1 red onion

Put all the orange-mustard dressing ingredients in a bowl, season to taste with freshly ground black pepper, then whisk together well. Cover and refrigerate for 15 minutes.

Meanwhile, cook the beans in boiling, salted water for 4 minutes, or until tender. Drain well, refresh under cold running water, then drain again. Pat dry with paper towels and toss in a large bowl with the baby spinach, watercress and tomatoes.

Preheat a barbecue grill plate or chargrill pan to medium–high. Brush the steaks with olive oil, then cook for 2 minutes on each side, or until still rare. Remove to a warmed plate, cover loosely with foil and leave to rest for 5 minutes.

Meanwhile, cut the onion in half, then into thin wedges. Brush with oil and chargrill over medium heat for 2–3 minutes on each side, or until softened and charred.

Thinly slice the beef across the grain. Arrange the salad mixture on a large platter, arrange the beef and onion over the top, then drizzle with the dressing. Sprinkle with sea salt and freshly ground black pepper and serve.

Carpetbag burgers with tarragon mayonnaise

Serves 6

TARRAGON MAYONNAISE
2 egg yolks, at room temperature
2 teaspoons dijon mustard
1 tablespoon tarragon vinegar, or to taste
200 ml (7 fl oz) olive oil
1 tablespoon finely chopped tarragon

750 g (1 lb 10 oz) minced (ground) beef
80 g (2¾ oz/1 cup) fresh white breadcrumbs
½ teaspoon finely grated lemon zest
5 drops of Tabasco sauce
1 egg, lightly beaten
6 oysters
olive oil, for brushing
6 good-quality hamburger buns
finely shredded lettuce, to serve

To make the tarragon mayonnaise, put the egg yolks, mustard and vinegar in a bowl and whisk together well. Whisking constantly, add the olive oil, a little at a time, making sure it is emulsified before adding more oil. Whisk until thick and creamy. Season to taste with sea salt and freshly ground black pepper, adding a little more vinegar if needed, then stir in the tarragon. Cover the surface of the mayonnaise directly with plastic wrap to prevent a skin forming.

To make the burgers, put the beef, breadcrumbs, lemon zest, Tabasco and egg in a large bowl and mix together well. Divide into six equal portions, then shape into patties 1.5 cm (⅝ inch) thick. With your thumb, make a cavity in the top of each burger. Place an oyster in the cavity and smooth the meat over to enclose the oyster completely. Refrigerate until required.

Heat a frying pan and brush lightly with olive oil. Cook the burgers on medium–high heat for 8 minutes on each side, turning only once.

Meanwhile, split the hamburger buns and lightly toast them, cut side up, under a hot grill (broiler). Keep warm.

Serve the burgers on the toasted buns with shredded lettuce and the tarragon mayonnaise.

lamb

Sheep belong to the same family (Bovidae) as goats and cattle and were among the very first animals to be domesticated. Early sheep were brown and hairy; over the centuries, many sheep breeds developed the woolly exterior we know today. Over time, some types lost their spectacularly curly horns, and their tails became shorter.

Easy to herd (unlike pigs), extremely hardy and able to survive on marginal land, the sheep has been an entirely useful animal, providing not just meat and wool, but also milk for delicious cheeses and yoghurt. For millennia, sheep were our principal source of meat — even today, to say 'meat' in the Middle East invariably means 'lamb' — and is the only red meat not subject to religious prohibitions. The ancient Sumerians had over 200 words to describe various characteristics of sheep and lamb. In many cultures, lambs were a crucial part of religious feasts and ceremonies, synonymous with innocence and purity. The lamb features heavily in the Bible and is used as a metaphor for Christ. It is an important food on the Jewish Passover table, is eaten by Muslims for their New Year and most other important occasions, and is traditionally eaten throughout Christendom at Easter.

Lamb was undoubtedly tougher then than today. Sheep were herded for long distances, and by the time of their slaughter would have been very lean and stringy indeed. Recipes from medieval days give laborious tenderising instructions, while those from ancient Rome see lamb wrapped in caul fat and stewed for hours in honey and milk, presumably to make it tender. In the Middle East, lamb was pounded finely before cooking, and the use of acid ingredients for marinating is still common there.

As early as the Renaissance, farmers began cross-breeding sheep to maximise meat and wool yields. In the eighteenth century, King Louis XV of France got in on the act; his son supposedly nicknamed his father's flocks 'walking cutlets'. In the same century, an Englishman named Robert Bakewell started experimenting with breeding to improve the meat yield of cattle and sheep, and so successful was he that he is credited as being the father of modern livestock breeding. Eventually the taste of mutton was greatly improved, and animals at slaughter were of a much greater size and quality.

In the United States, lamb consumption is rather low, perhaps due to the historic prevalence of beef, and a belief that lamb is unpleasantly strong-tasting. Sheep, in contrast, have always been vital to the British economy; for centuries wool and textile exports were its very backbone. It is believed long-wool types of sheep were introduced to Britain by the Romans, although other breeds probably came with the Viking invaders.

There are now many hundreds of varieties of domesticated sheep — wool breeds, fat-tailed breeds (prevalent in the Middle East, arid parts of Africa and Central Asia, bred for their meat, tail fat and wool), haired breeds (found in tropical places such as the Caribbean and used for their meat), and the stocky, somewhat square-shaped meat breeds that most of us think of when we think 'sheep'. Some are quite exotic (the Chinese Tong, Dutch Zwartbles, Afghan Turki or Flemish Voskop) while others, such as the Merino, Romney and Corriedale, are ubiquitous, ranging in their millions upon millions over green hillsides of the world.

LAMB, HOGGET, MUTTON — WHAT'S THE DIFFERENCE?

'Lamb' is technically meat from a sheep slaughtered under one year of age; in New Zealand, the animal is required to have 'no permanent incisors in wear'. Once a lamb has two incisors, it is considered hogget (called 'yearling' in America). Meat from sheep over two years old is classified as mutton.

In regional Spain, milk-fed lamb is particularly popular; this is lamb still suckled by its mother and aged only 4–6 weeks at slaughter. Rome is similarly famed for its *abbacchio* (see page 82), or baby spring lamb. Spring lamb is generally 3–5 months old when slaughtered and is highly sought after for its very sweet, succulent meat. France produces one of the world's finest lambs, called *pré-salé*, which is raised on the salt marshes of Brittany and Normandy. It has a singular flavour, as does Australian saltbush lamb, which forages on a drought-hardy plant called saltbush whose leaves have a strong, salty tang.

In the United States, most lamb is grass fed, then finished on grain for a few months before slaughter; this results in a heavy carcass with mild-tasting, somewhat fatty meat. Australian and New Zealand lambs, on the other hand, are all pasture-raised and eat only grass; at slaughter they are smaller but have sweet, mellow meat that is not so fatty.

Like cattle, sheep are ruminants, designed to survive on pasture and other grass-derived forage such as hay. Grain-feeding can upset their finely tuned digestion, and being housed in intensive feed-lots creates the same potential hazards as any animal raised in such a way: namely, those related to stress, disease and the accumulation of large amounts of waste. There is a growing trend towards 'naturally' raised meats and in the case of lamb, this simply equates to grass fed. On the whole though, because of their hardy, adaptable nature, sheep have pretty much escaped the highly intensive farming scenarios so common with other animals and poultry.

Hanging lamb

Like beef, lamb is hung for aging, but because it ages quickly it is hung for a much shorter time — only up to a week, although 3 days is normally sufficient. (For more on dry-aging, see page 23.) However, because of the economic inducements involved in getting meat to market quickly, much of the lamb we buy is offered for sale within just 3 days of slaughter. The meat from older sheep doesn't benefit from hanging as the tough connective tissues will not soften — the meat requires long, slow cooking to become tender.

pH levels in lamb

Levels of pH greatly influence a meat's tenderness and flavour. Very high pH in lamb causes strong odours and changes its flavour; the meat is also tougher and spoils faster than meat with a lower pH. Stress greatly increases pH, so careful management prior to slaughter is required to minimise this. Toughness in lamb can also be caused by what is called 'cold-shortening', that is, too-quick chilling after slaughter, shocking the muscles into a tough state that can't be reversed by any amount of aging. For all these reasons, it is essential to buy lamb from a reputable supplier.

Nutritional content

Lamb is high in conjugated linoleic acid (CLA), which may help combat diabetes, reduce the risk of clogged arteries and inhibit cancer cells. Lambs fed grass contain more CLA (and less fat) than grain-fed lamb; they are also higher in vitamin E, omega-3 fatty acids and beta-carotene. Lamb contains good quantities of selenium, zinc, vitamin B12, niacin and phosphorous.

Choosing lamb

The younger the lamb, the lighter the colour of the meat; the size and weight of the cuts will also give a rough guide to age. Lamb meat should be a fresh, light red with a firm, fine texture, sweet smell and have white, dry-to-the-touch fat. Bones ought to be pink and moist with porous ends; avoid lamb with dried-out, white bones or with fat that is going yellow. (Mutton, however, will have purplish flesh, a strong sheepy odour and white bones.)

Avoid lamb with browning or tacky-feeling meat or blood spots in the flesh. Lamb fat may still be covered in a dry, parchment-type 'skin' called 'fell' when you buy it, although these days it is likely to be removed before sale. The fell, which is a membrane between the skin and the flesh, helps larger pieces of lamb such as roasts keep their shape while cooking and you don't actually need to remove it. Do, however, take it off small cuts like chops as it shrinks slightly during cooking and can distort their shape.

Storage

Lamb will keep, stored in the coolest part of the refrigerator, for 3–4 days. As a general rule, meat on the bone will not last quite as long as meat off the bone. Minced (ground) lamb, which has had more opportunity to come into contact with bacteria, will only last for 2 days. Take the meat out of any packaging, place it on a tray or plate and cover it with fresh plastic wrap; mince can be placed in a covered bowl or container. Drain off any bloody juices that collect as these can turn sour and taint the meat.

Lamb can also be frozen for up to 6 months, well wrapped in several layers of thick plastic to protect it from freezer burn; however, it is better consumed within 3 months. Frozen minced lamb will last 4 months.

Cuts of lamb

To understand its construction, think of a lamb as having four quarters.

A forequarter section comprises the neck and shoulder; directly behind these is the rib (or rack) portion. Under these cuts are the foreleg (which yields a shank) and the breast, which can be sold and cooked still on its ribs, or boned and rolled (in some countries it is then called a lamb flap).

The hindquarter has the loin (along with the rib it is the most tender part), the leg and the hind shank.

Generally, the minced (ground) lamb sold in most supermarkets and butcher shops will be taken from inferior cuts and can be fatty. It is much better to grind your own — buy a boned shoulder or leg and chop it finely yourself by hand, or pass it through a mincing attachment of an electric mixer or an old-fashioned crank-style meat grinder (see page 13).

COOKING LAMB

Lamb is eaten the world over and features in the barbecues of Mongolia, the kebabs of Turkey, the curries of India, tagines of Morocco and hotpots of Britain. Because lamb is such a young meat, most parts of it are suited to fast, dry-heat cooking. The shoulder, which can be roasted, also makes a tasty braise as it is full of connective tissue. The leg, so popular for roasting, can also be cut to yield steaks and cutlets, which are highly suited to frying or grilling. The leg can also be poached, braised or slow-roasted under cover for up to 8 hours. Whole lamb carcasses, or smaller cuts such as a leg, can be spit-roasted. There are myriad recipes for braises, stews or very long, slow roasts that produce moist, fall-apart meat of utmost tenderness. Minced (ground) lamb features in dishes like moussaka, shepherd's pie and Middle Eastern meatballs. The Lebanese make an art of *kibbi naya* — scrupulously trimmed lean lamb, finely chopped by hand, then served raw.

Lamb lends itself to so many flavours. Mint is a classic partner, but lamb is equally good with rosemary, thyme, dill, parsley and oregano. In North Africa it is cooked with warm spices (saffron, cumin, cinnamon, coriander) and fruit (apricots, quince, prunes). Lamb and lemon are a time-honoured pairing, and its richness also suits the tartness of tamarind, pomegranate molasses or good vinegar. The pungent flavours of garlic, anchovies and preserved lemons are also excellent partners. Lamb loves red or white wine, is excellent with beans, chickpeas, lentils and olives, and has a special affinity for garlic, spinach and eggplant (aubergine). Rice, couscous, potatoes and burghul (bulgar) are excellent accompaniments.

Braising

The classic lamb cut for braising is the shank. Years ago it was considered a cheap off-cut, but has enjoyed a titanic surge in popularity (and price) on restaurant menus. Like any meat cooked on the bone, the shank is extremely flavoursome — its large quantities of connective tissue give it a wonderful, lip-smacking quality when cooked to fall-off-the-bone tenderness.

Ask your butcher to 'french' the shanks (cutting back and trimming the bone clean for a neater appearance), then braise them in the oven in a large, wide saucepan or a deep roasting dish, covered tightly with foil. Most cooks don't bother to make lamb stock for lamb braises; generally veal or chicken stocks are used (beef stock is too strong). Wine can be added, as can all manner of flavourings — herbs, spices, dried beans, fruits and vegetables.

The breast and shoulder (including shoulder chops) are also suited to braising. If cooking the meat from hogget or mutton, the neck (cut into chops or into pieces) and leg (cut into small chunks) will also be good braised.

Roasting

Roasted lamb is a great celebratory meal everywhere from Greece, Ireland and Italy to Iran, Israel, New Zealand and Mexico. Arguably the best cut to roast is the leg, although the French make much of a roasted shoulder (fattier but very flavoursome). The rack of lamb, also called the best end of neck, presents elegantly with its neat row of bones (an entire rack has 13 bones, while a smaller-cut rack will typically have eight). If roasting racks of lamb, make sure the bones are 'frenched' (trimmed cleanly of every scrap of meat) for a neater appearance at the table. Also, to stop the bones from charring, wrap them in foil before roasting, and remove the foil for serving.

The saddle — essentially the two loins still attached in the middle — also makes a sensational roast. The boned-out breast, also called the 'flap', is an economical cut to roast (have it rolled and tied by your butcher), and these days there are other smaller, lean roasts available — prime pieces from the leg such as the rump and round (or topside), and the boned-out loin. The neck, sometimes called the rib-eye roast, is also good.

An entire leg or shoulder can be boned and stuffed before roasting — it's best to get your butcher to bone these for you.

Whether roasting lamb on or off the bone, the same basic rules apply. For fast roasting, place the meat in a roasting tin, rub all over with olive oil and season well. If you like, make slits all over the surface of the roast using a small, sharp knife, and insert chopped garlic, rosemary or anchovies into the incisions for extra flavour. Place in a 220°C (425°F/Gas 7) oven and roast until done. Use a meat thermometer to determine the point of 'doneness' — 60°C (140°F) for medium–rare, 65–70°C (150–158°F) for medium and 80°C (175°F) for well done. Some cooks pour a little boiling water into the roasting dish after 30 minutes, then baste the roast every so often with the juices; these pan juices then form the basis of a gravy or jus when the meat is cooked. Others place the meat directly onto an oven rack and place a pan with some liquid in it a few rungs under the meat.

To slow-roast lamb, use the same procedure, except reduce the oven temperature to 170°C (325°F/Gas 3) after 30 minutes and cook until done.

Remember to loosely cover and rest the lamb in a warm spot after cooking — this is vital for a juicy roast.

Grilling, barbecuing, pan-frying

Chops, cutlets and 'steaks' cut from muscles such as the rump or topside are made for grilling and frying, with their good dispersion of fat and sweet flesh that cooks to chewy, golden perfection on the outside. Avoid thin cutlets — they should be at least 2.5–3 cm (1–1¼ inches) thick.

The most tender cutlets come from the rib and loin; rib chops carry more fat than loin chops. Shoulder chops can be grilled, but vary in quality and tenderness; they can benefit from marinating first, as will leg chops.

Use either a barbecue or a cast-iron ridged chargrill pan to grill, and a heavy-based cast-iron pan to fry. These cuts can also be cooked under an oven grill (broiler), although the very tender loin and rib chops are best for this and should be cooked very close to the element.

Cook these tender cuts as quickly as you can, without burning. Trim off the excess fat, but leave a good edge of it around the meat for flavour and lubrication. Brush the lamb well with olive oil to stop it sticking and cook for 1–2 minutes on each side to seal it. If your meat is no more than 2.5 cm (1 inch) thick, this length of time, with a 5-minute rest, may well be enough to cook the meat to medium–rare. (Grilled or fried lamb is best served medium–rare, or medium at most, or it will be tough and uninteresting.)

Chops and cutlets can be lightly crumbed and fried or, when a small pocket is cut into their side, filled with a savoury stuffing. Choose stuffing ingredients that don't require cooking through — chopped sun-dried tomatoes, capers and parmesan cheese for flavour, with breadcrumbs as a base.

Poaching

Many cuts of lamb are suitable for this gentle method of cooking. The shoulder, breast, shank and neck are all prime candidates, with their rich loads of connective tissue and lubricating layers or strands of fat. Long, gentle cooking break these down to make the meat soft and moist.

A lamb leg, although it doesn't contain as much connective tissue, is also excellent to poach as the internal fat networks ensure it remains juicy, especially if it isn't cooked beyond medium–rare. Don't cook it all the way through or it will be terribly grey and uninteresting.

Choose a saucepan large enough to hold the lamb snugly. Add water (or chicken stock) to cover, some aromatic vegetables (celery, onion, carrot, leeks, garlic) and herbs (thyme, bay leaves, rosemary), then bring to a simmer. Add the meat — if using a leg, tie it at 5 cm (2 inch) intervals with string to keep a neat shape — then bring the liquid just back to the simmer. Adjust the heat so that the liquid barely murmurs (bubbles shouldn't break the surface). A leg should register 62°C (145°F) for medium–rare and 65°C (150°F) for medium when ready; neck, shoulder, breast or shanks should have an internal temperature of 70°C (158°F) for well done.

Once the meat is cooked, the skimmed, strained liquid can be served as a broth or made into a heartier soup — you can also thicken some of it with egg yolks and serve it as a sauce with the lamb.

Harira (chickpea, lamb and coriander soup)

Serves 4–6

- 2 tablespoons olive oil
- 2 small onions, chopped
- 2 large garlic cloves, crushed
- 500 g (1 lb 2 oz) lamb shoulder steaks, trimmed of excess fat and sinew, cut into small cubes
- 1½ teaspoons ground cumin
- 2 teaspoons paprika
- ½ teaspoon ground cloves
- 1 bay leaf
- 2 tablespoons tomato paste (concentrated purée)
- 1 litre (35 fl oz/4 cups) beef stock
- 3 x 300 g (10½ oz) tins chickpeas, rinsed and drained
- 800 g (1 lb 12 oz) tin good-quality chopped tomatoes
- 2–3 handfuls coriander (cilantro), finely chopped
- extra virgin olive oil, to serve
- coriander (cilantro) leaves, to garnish
- small black olives, to garnish
- toasted pitta bread, to serve

Heat the olive oil in a large, heavy-based saucepan or stockpot. Add the onion and garlic and sauté over medium heat for 5 minutes, or until softened. Add the lamb in batches and cook over medium heat for 4–5 minutes, turning to brown all over. Return all the lamb to the pan with the spices and bay leaf and stir until fragrant.

Add the tomato paste and cook for 2 minutes, stirring constantly. Add the stock, chickpeas, tomato and chopped coriander, stir well and bring to the boil. Reduce the heat, then cover and simmer, stirring occasionally, for 2 hours, or until the lamb is tender. Season to taste with sea salt and freshly ground black pepper.

Divide the soup among warmed bowls and drizzle with a little extra virgin olive oil. Scatter with coriander leaves and olives and serve with toasted pitta bread.

Lamb stuffed with olives, feta and oregano

Serves 4

OLIVE AND GARLIC PASTE
85 g (3 oz/½ cup) pitted kalamata olives
3 garlic cloves, crushed
2 tablespoons olive oil

800 g (1 lb 12 oz) lamb backstraps or loin fillets, trimmed
100 g (3½ oz/⅔ cup) crumbled feta cheese
2 tablespoons finely shredded oregano
4 tablespoons lemon juice
3 tablespoons olive oil

Put all the olive and garlic paste ingredients in a food processor or blender and blend until smooth. Season to taste with freshly ground black pepper.

Prepare the lamb by cutting horizontally most of the way through the fillets, starting at one end and leaving a small join at the other end. Open out the lamb so you have a piece roughly half as thick and twice as long as you started with.

Spread the olive and garlic paste in a thin, even layer over the cut surface of the lamb, then sprinkle the feta and oregano over the top. Roll the lamb up tightly, starting with one of the long cut edges, and tie the whole length with kitchen string, so that the filling is contained and secure.

Put the lamb into a dish large enough to hold it lying flat and drizzle with the lemon juice and olive oil, turning to coat well. Cover and refrigerate for 3 hours.

Preheat a barbecue chargrill plate or chargrill pan to medium–high. Season the lamb with sea salt and freshly ground black pepper, then cook, turning to brown each side, for about 10 minutes for medium–rare, or until cooked to your liking. Transfer to a plate, cover loosely with foil and leave to rest in a warm place for 10 minutes.

Using a large, sharp knife, cut the lamb on the diagonal into 5 cm (2 inch) pieces and serve.

Lamb shanks with chickpeas

Serves 4

1 tablespoon extra virgin olive oil
4 large or 8 small lamb shanks
2 onions, finely chopped
2 garlic cloves, crushed
1 tablespoon harissa (see Note), plus extra, to serve (optional)
1 cinnamon stick
2 x 400 g (14 oz) tins chopped tomatoes
2 x 300 g (10½ oz) tins chickpeas, rinsed and drained
90 g (3¼ oz/½ cup) green olives
½ tablespoon preserved lemon rind or lemon zest, finely chopped
2 tablespoons mint, chopped
steamed couscous, to serve

Heat the olive oil in a large flameproof casserole dish over medium heat. Add the shanks and cook for 7–8 minutes, turning to brown all over. Remove the shanks from the dish and set aside.

Add the onion and garlic to the casserole dish and sauté for 2–3 minutes, or until the onion starts to soften. Add the harissa and cinnamon stick and season with sea salt and freshly ground black pepper. Stir well, then add the tomatoes and the shanks and bring to the boil, adding a little water if needed so the shanks are covered with liquid. Cover, reduce the heat to low and simmer for 50 minutes.

Stir in the chickpeas, olives and preserved lemon. Season to taste with sea salt and freshly ground black pepper and cook, uncovered, for a further 20–30 minutes, or until the lamb is very tender and almost falling off the bone. Skim the fat off the sauce, then stir in the mint.

Serve the shanks and chickpeas on a bed of steamed couscous, with extra harissa passed separately if desired.

NOTE: Harissa is an intensely hot chilli-based paste that is widely used in North African cooking. You will find it in specialist food stores and good delicatessens.

Lamb, bean and potato salad with almond garlic sauce

Serves 6

800 g (1 lb 12 oz) small boiling potatoes, peeled
600 g (1 lb 5 oz) green beans, trimmed
2 tablespoons olive oil
800 g (1 lb 12 oz) lamb backstraps or loin fillets, trimmed
100 g (3½ oz/½ cup) small black olives
120 g (4¼ oz/4 cups) watercress sprigs
90 g (3¼ oz/1 bunch) coriander (cilantro), leaves picked

ALMOND GARLIC SAUCE
1 egg yolk
2 tablespoons ground almonds
4 garlic cloves, crushed
1½ teaspoons dijon mustard
1½ tablespoons white wine vinegar
60 ml (2 fl oz/¼ cup) walnut oil

Preheat the oven to 200°C (400°F/Gas 6). Put the potatoes in a saucepan, cover with water and bring to the boil. Cook for 10 minutes, or until tender. Remove from the saucepan with a slotted spoon and set aside.

Add the beans to the boiling water and cook for 4 minutes, or until tender. Remove from the saucepan, refresh under cold running water, then drain well and set aside.

Heat the olive oil in a large, heavy-based ovenproof frying pan until very hot. Season the lamb with sea salt and freshly ground black pepper and sear for 1 minute on each side, then transfer the pan to the oven and roast the lamb for 8–10 minutes, or until cooked but still pink in the middle. Remove the lamb to a plate and allow to cool to room temperature.

Thinly slice the lamb on the diagonal and place in a large bowl. Slice the cooled potatoes and add to the lamb with the remaining salad ingredients.

To make the almond garlic sauce, put the egg yolk, ground almonds, garlic, mustard and vinegar in a mini food processor, then blend until smooth and well combined. With the motor running, add the walnut oil a teaspoon or so at time, until a smooth, thick sauce forms. Slowly add 2 tablespoons boiling water and blend just until well combined; the sauce should be thick and smooth. Season to taste with sea salt and freshly ground black pepper.

Add enough sauce to the salad to just coat, tossing well. Divide among plates or shallow bowls, drizzle with a little more of the sauce and serve the remaining sauce separately.

Lamb in the pot with juniper berries

Serves 6

1 tablespoon olive oil
1 onion, finely chopped
2 garlic cloves, finely chopped
1 carrot, diced
1 celery stalk, diced
2 bay leaves
310 ml (10¾ fl oz/1¼ cups) dry white wine
125 ml (4 fl oz/½ cup) chicken stock
30 juniper berries
1 teaspoon chopped rosemary
1.5 kg (3 lb 5 oz) leg of lamb
1 tablespoon balsamic vinegar

Heat the olive oil in a large, heavy-based saucepan over medium heat. Add the onion, garlic, carrot and celery and sauté for 5 minutes, or until the onion is lightly coloured.

Add the bay leaves, wine, stock, juniper berries, rosemary and lamb leg and bring to the boil. Reduce the heat to low, cover with a tight-fitting lid and simmer gently for 2½ hours, or until the lamb is very tender and nearly falling off the bone.

Transfer the lamb leg to a warmed plate, cover loosely with foil and rest in a warm place for 10 minutes.

Add the vinegar to the saucepan and simmer over medium heat for several minutes until the sauce has reduced and thickened. Season to taste with sea salt and freshly ground black pepper.

Carve the lamb, arrange on warmed plates and serve drizzled with the sauce.

Mechoui

Serves 6

2 kg (4 lb 8 oz) leg of lamb
75 g (2½ oz) butter, softened
3 garlic cloves, crushed
2 teaspoons ground cumin
3 teaspoons ground coriander
1 teaspoon paprika
¼ teaspoon sea salt

SPICE MIX
1 tablespoon ground cumin
1½ teaspoons sea salt

Preheat the oven to 220°C (425°F/Gas 7). Using a small, sharp knife, make incisions 1 cm (½ inch) deep all over the lamb.

Put the butter, garlic and spices in a bowl and mix to a smooth paste. Using the back of a spoon, rub the paste all over the lamb, pushing it into the incisions, making sure the lamb is completely covered with the paste.

Sit the lamb leg in a deep roasting tin and place on the top shelf of the oven. Roast for 10 minutes, then baste with the pan juices and return to the oven. Reduce the oven temperature to 150°C (300°F/Gas 2). Roast for a further 3 hours 20 minutes, or until the lamb is very tender, basting every 20–30 minutes. Transfer to a plate, cover loosely with foil and leave to rest in a warm place for 10 minutes.

Carve the lamb into chunky pieces. Combine the spice mix ingredients in a small bowl and serve on the side for dipping into.

Roast lamb

Serves 6

- 2 rosemary sprigs
- 3 garlic cloves, chopped
- 75 g (2½ oz) pancetta, chopped
- 2 kg (4 lb 8 oz) leg of lamb, shank bone cut off just above the joint, then trimmed of excess fat and tied
- 1 large onion
- 125 ml (4 fl oz/½ cup) olive oil
- 375 ml (13 fl oz/1½ cups) dry white wine

Preheat the oven to 230°C (450°F/Gas 8). Pull the leaves off the rosemary sprigs. Using a large, sharp knife, chop the rosemary, garlic and pancetta until a coarse paste forms, then season with sea salt and freshly ground black pepper.

Using a small, sharp knife, make incisions 1 cm (½ inch) deep all over the lamb. Rub the rosemary mixture over the lamb, pushing it into the incisions.

Peel the onion, then cut it widthways into four thick slices and place in the centre of a roasting tin. Sit the lamb leg on top, pour the olive oil over, then roast for 15 minutes.

Reduce the oven temperature to 180°C (350°F/Gas 4) and pour in 250 ml (9 fl oz/1 cup) of the wine. Roast for 1¼ hours for medium–rare, or until cooked to your liking, basting from time to time and adding a little water if the juices start to burn. Transfer the lamb leg to a warm platter, cover loosely with foil and leave to rest in a warm place for 10 minutes.

Remove the onion from the roasting tin and spoon off the excess fat. Place over high heat on the stovetop, pour in the remaining wine and cook for 3–4 minutes, or until the sauce reduces and thickens. Season to taste.

Carve the lamb, arrange on warmed plates and serve with the sauce spooned over the top.

Lamb filo rolls

Makes 12

FILLING

1 tablespoon olive oil
350 g (12 oz) minced (ground) lamb
1 small onion, finely chopped
2 garlic cloves, crushed
1 tablespoon ground cumin
1 teaspoon ground ginger
1 teaspoon paprika
1 teaspoon ground cinnamon
a pinch of saffron threads, soaked in a little warm water
2 tablespoons chopped coriander (cilantro) leaves
2 tablespoons chopped flat-leaf (Italian) parsley
1 teaspoon harissa (see Note on page 65)
3 tablespoons pine nuts, toasted
1 egg

6 sheets of filo pastry
60 g (2¼ oz) butter, melted
1 tablespoon sesame seeds
lemon wedges, to serve

Preheat the oven to 180°C (350°F/Gas 4). Lightly grease a large baking tray.

To make the filling, heat the olive oil in a large frying pan, add the lamb and cook for 5 minutes, breaking up any lumps with the back of a wooden spoon. Add the onion and garlic and cook for 1 minute. Add the spices, herbs and harissa and cook for 1 minute, stirring to combine. Transfer the mixture to a sieve to drain off the excess fat.

Place the mixture in a bowl and leave to cool slightly. Mix in the pine nuts and egg.

Place a sheet of filo pastry on a work surface with a short side facing you. Cover the remaining sheets with a damp tea towel (dish towel) to stop them drying out. Cut the sheet of pastry lengthways into four equal strips. Brush one of the strips with melted butter and place another on top. Repeat with the remaining two pieces so you have two long pieces of pastry. Place 1 tablespoon of the filling at the short end of each piece of pastry and roll up, tucking in the ends to hold the mixture in, and form each into a cigar shape. Repeat with the remaining filo sheets and filling.

Place the filo rolls on the baking tray. Brush with any remaining melted butter and sprinkle with the sesame seeds. Bake for 15 minutes, or until lightly golden. Serve warm, with lemon wedges.

Lamb braised with flageolet beans

Serves 4

125 g (4½ oz/⅔ cup) dried flageolet or haricot beans, soaked overnight and drained (see Note)
1 kg (2 lb 4 oz) boned shoulder of lamb, tied with string to keep its shape
30 g (1 oz) clarified butter
2 carrots, diced
2 large onions, chopped
4 garlic cloves, unpeeled
1 bouquet garni
250 ml (9 fl oz/1 cup) dry red wine
250 ml (9 fl oz/1 cup) veal or chicken stock

Put the beans in a large saucepan of cold unsalted water. Bring to the boil, then reduce the heat and simmer, partially covered, for 50–60 minutes, or until tender. Drain well.

Rub the lamb all over with sea salt and freshly ground black pepper. Melt the butter over high heat in a large, flameproof casserole dish. Add the lamb and cook for 8–10 minutes, turning to brown all over. Remove the lamb and set aside.

Add the carrot, onion, garlic and bouquet garni to the casserole dish. Reduce the heat and cook, stirring, for 8–10 minutes, or until the vegetables have softened. Increase the heat to high and pour in the wine. Boil for 30 seconds, stirring to loosen any bits stuck to the bottom of the dish, then put the lamb back in. Add the stock, bring to the boil, then cover with a tight-fitting lid and reduce the heat to low. Simmer for 1½ hours, turning the lamb twice. Add the beans, then cover and cook for a further 30 minutes.

Transfer the lamb to a plate, cover loosely with foil and leave to rest in a warm place for 10 minutes.

Discard the bouquet garni from the sauce and skim off the excess fat. If the sauce is too thin, boil it over high heat for 5 minutes, or until thickened slightly. Season to taste with sea salt and freshly ground black pepper.

Carve the lamb and serve on warmed plates with the beans and sauce spooned over the top.

NOTE: You can buy flageolet beans from delicatessens and speciality grocers. These tiny French kidney beans have a delicate flavour and are a classic accompaniment to lamb.

Cassoulet

Serves 6

400 g (14 oz/2 cups) dried haricot beans, soaked overnight and drained
1 bouquet garni
½ large onion, cut into quarters
2 garlic cloves, crushed
200 g (7 oz) salt pork or unsmoked bacon, cut into cubes
1 tablespoon clarified butter
375 g (13 oz) lamb shoulder, cut into 8 pieces (have your butcher do this)
4 boiling sausages, about 350 g (12 oz) in total
1 celery stalk, sliced
4 pieces of duck confit (see page 219), or 4 roasted duck pieces
6 large tomatoes
2 Toulouse sausages, about 175 g (6 oz) in total, or any good-quality fresh pork sausages
4 baguette slices, made into crumbs

Put the beans in a large saucepan with the bouquet garni, onion, garlic and salt pork. Add enough cold water to cover and bring to the boil, skimming off any scum that rises to the surface. Reduce the heat and simmer for 1 hour.

Heat the butter in a frying pan. Add the lamb and cook over medium–high heat for 5–6 minutes, turning to brown all over. Add to the beans with the boiling sausages, celery and duck confit, pushing them into the liquid to submerge them. (Don't wash the frying pan yet as you'll need it later.)

Using a small, sharp knife, score a small cross in the base of each tomato. Plunge into boiling water for 20 seconds, then remove and plunge into iced water to cool. Peel the skin away from the cross, then chop the tomatoes finely, discarding the cores. Add the chopped tomatoes to the cassoulet, pushing them into the liquid. Cook for a further 1 hour.

Brown the Toulouse sausages in the same frying pan the lamb was browned in and add to the cassoulet. Push them down into the liquid and cook for 30 minutes more.

Meanwhile, preheat the oven to 160°C (315°F/Gas 2–3). Remove the bouquet garni from the cassoulet. Strain the liquid into a saucepan and boil over moderate heat until reduced by two-thirds. Remove all the meat from the bean mixture, then slice the sausages and pull the duck meat from the bones. Layer the meat and beans, alternately, in a deep casserole dish. Pour in enough of the liquid to just cover the beans.

Sprinkle the cassoulet with the breadcrumbs and bake for 40 minutes. Every 10 minutes, break the breadcrumb crust with the back of a spoon to let a little liquid come through. If the beans look dry, add a little stock or water to the edge of the dish. Serve hot, straight from the casserole dish.

Navarin of lamb

Serves 6

- 1.25 kg (2 lb 12 oz) boned lamb shoulder or leg
- 4 tablespoons olive oil
- 1 tablespoon plain (all-purpose) flour
- 2 tablespoons tomato paste (concentrated purée)
- 750 ml (26 fl oz/3 cups) chicken stock
- 500 ml (17 fl oz/2 cups) lamb stock
- 3 slices of bacon, chopped
- 1 onion, chopped
- 2 carrots, roughly chopped
- 3 garlic cloves, crushed
- 1 leek, white part only, rinsed well and roughly chopped
- 10 spring onions (scallions), white part only, chopped
- 1 tablespoon chopped thyme
- 700 g (1 lb 9 oz) desiree or other all-purpose potatoes, peeled and sliced

Preheat the oven to 160°C (315°F/Gas 2–3). Trim the lamb and cut into 5 cm (2 inch) chunks.

Heat half the olive oil in a large frying pan. Add the lamb in batches and cook over medium heat for 4–5 minutes, turning to brown all over. Return all the lamb to the pan, add the flour and tomato paste and stir to combine. Gradually pour in all the stock, stirring constantly. Bring the mixture to a simmer, cook for 1 minute, or until the liquid has thickened, then transfer to a large flameproof casserole dish.

Clean the frying pan and heat the remaining olive oil. Add the bacon, onion, carrot, garlic and leek and sauté over medium heat for 8 minutes, or until the onion is golden. Add the mixture to the casserole dish with the spring onion and thyme. Cover and bake for 1 hour.

Remove the casserole from the oven and skim the fat from the surface of the sauce. Season to taste with sea salt and freshly ground black pepper, then overlap the potato slices in the dish, covering the surface with a thick layer. Cover and bake for a further 45 minutes, or until the potato is tender.

Increase the oven temperature to 180°C (350°F/Gas 4), remove the casserole lid and bake for a further 25 minutes, or until the potato is golden.

Lamb kibbeh

Serves 6

235 g (8½ oz/1⅓ cups) burghul (bulgur)
500 g (1 lb 2 oz) minced (ground) lean lamb
2 onions, finely chopped
2 teaspoons ground allspice
1 teaspoon sea salt
1 teaspoon freshly ground black pepper
1 tablespoon pine nuts
4 tablespoons ghee, melted
green salad, to serve
hummus, to serve
large pitta breads, to serve

FILLING
1 tablespoon ghee
1 small onion, finely chopped
1 teaspoon ground allspice
½ teaspoon freshly ground black pepper
1 teaspoon ground nutmeg
250 g (9 oz) minced (ground) lamb
80 g (2¾ oz/½ cup) pine nuts

Put the burghul in a bowl, cover with cold water and leave to soak for about 15 minutes. Drain well. Using your hands, squeeze out as much liquid as possible.

Put the burghul in a bowl with the lamb, onion, allspice, salt and pepper. Knead the mixture with 100 ml (3½ fl oz) iced water until a fine paste forms.

To make the filling, heat the ghee in a frying pan over medium heat. Add the onion and spices and sauté for 3 minutes, or until the onion has softened. Add the lamb and sauté for 5 minutes, or until the mixture has changed colour. Stir in the pine nuts and season to taste with sea salt and freshly ground black pepper. Set aside to cool slightly.

Meanwhile, preheat the oven to 180°C (350°F/Gas 4).

Lightly grease a 30 cm (12 inch) oval baking dish with a 2 litre (70 fl oz/8 cup) capacity. Press half the burghul and lamb mixture over the base, top with the filling, and press the remaining lamb mixture over the top. Using a sharp knife, score 4 cm (1½ inch) diamond shapes through the kibbeh. Press a pine nut in the centre of each diamond.

Drizzle the kibbeh with the melted ghee and bake for 1½ hours, or until cooked through, covering it with foil if it becomes too brown.

Cut the kibbeh into diamonds and serve with a green salad, hummus and pitta bread.

Rack of lamb with herb crust

SERVES 4

2 x 6-cutlet racks of lamb, French-trimmed (ask your butcher to do this)
1 tablespoon olive oil
80 g (2¾ oz/1 cup) fresh white breadcrumbs
3 garlic cloves, crushed
3 tablespoons finely chopped flat-leaf (Italian) parsley
½ tablespoon thyme
½ teaspoon finely grated lemon zest
60 g (2¼ oz) butter, softened

THYME AND GARLIC SAUCE
250 ml (9 fl oz/1 cup) beef stock
1 garlic clove, finely chopped
1 thyme sprig

Preheat the oven to 250°C (500°F/Gas 9). Score the fat on the lamb racks in a diamond pattern. Rub the lamb with a little of the olive oil and season with sea salt and freshly ground black pepper.

Heat the remaining olive oil in a frying pan over high heat. Add the lamb racks and brown them for 4–5 minutes (you may need to brown them one at a time). Remove and set aside (don't wash the pan yet as you'll need it later).

Combine the breadcrumbs, garlic, parsley, thyme and lemon zest in a large bowl, season to taste, then mix in the butter to form a paste.

Firmly press a layer of the breadcrumb mixture over the layer of fat on the lamb racks, taking care to leave the bones and base clean. Place the racks in a roasting tin and roast for 12 minutes for medium–rare, or until cooked to your liking. Transfer to a warmed plate, cover loosely with foil and leave to rest in a warm place.

To make the thyme and garlic sauce, add the stock, garlic and thyme sprig to the roasting tin juices, stirring to loosen any bits stuck to the bottom of the pan. Return this liquid to the reserved frying pan and simmer over high heat for 5–8 minutes, or until the sauce has thickened and reduced.

Strain the sauce and serve with the lamb racks.

Lemon and coriander baked lamb

Serves 4–6

1.8 kg (4 lb) leg of lamb
2 garlic cloves, sliced
3 large strips of lemon rind, cut into 1 cm (1/2 inch) pieces
a handful of chopped coriander (cilantro)
3 tablespoons chopped flat-leaf (Italian) parsley
2 tablespoons olive oil
1 teaspoon freshly ground black pepper

WHITE BEAN PURÉE

2 x 400 g (14 oz) tins cannellini beans, rinsed and drained
100 g (3 1/2 oz/1 cup) ground almonds
1 tablespoon lemon juice
3 garlic cloves, chopped
125 ml (4 fl oz/1/2 cup) olive oil
1 teaspoon finely chopped oregano

Preheat the oven to 180°C (350°F/Gas 4). Trim the lamb of excess fat and sinew. Using a small, sharp knife, make incisions 1 cm (1/2 inch) deep all over the lamb, then place a slice of garlic and a piece of lemon rind in each incision.

Combine the coriander, parsley, olive oil and pepper in a bowl, then rub the mixture all over the lamb. Place the lamb on a rack in a roasting tin and pour 250 ml (9 fl oz/1 cup) water into the tin. Bake for 1 hour 20 minutes, or until the lamb is cooked but still a little pink in the middle — add extra water to the tin during cooking if necessary.

Transfer the lamb to a warmed plate, cover loosely with foil and leave to rest in a warm place for 10–15 minutes.

Meanwhile, make the white bean purée. Put the beans, almonds, lemon juice and garlic in a food processor and blend until smooth. With the motor running, add the olive oil in a thin stream and process until thick and creamy.

Transfer to a saucepan, then stir over low heat until heated through. Season to taste with sea salt and freshly ground black pepper and stir in the oregano.

Carve the lamb, arrange on warmed plates and serve with the pan juices and white bean purée.

Rosemary lamb on grilled polenta with anchovy sauce

Serves 4

1 tablespoon finely chopped rosemary
3 garlic cloves, bruised
2 tablespoons olive oil
1 tablespoon lemon juice
600 g (1 lb 5 oz) lamb backstraps or loin fillets, trimmed
rocket (arugula) leaves, to serve

POLENTA
250 g (9 oz/1⅔ cups) instant polenta
4 tablespoons grated parmesan cheese
20 g (¾ oz) butter

ANCHOVY SAUCE
8 large anchovy fillets, chopped
3 teaspoons finely chopped rosemary
150 ml (5 fl oz) olive oil
1 tablespoon lemon juice

Combine the rosemary, garlic, olive oil and lemon juice in a non-metallic bowl. Add the lamb, turning to coat. Season with freshly ground black pepper, then cover and refrigerate for at least 4 hours, or preferably overnight.

Meanwhile, make the polenta. Bring 1 litre (35 fl oz/ 4 cups) salted water to the boil in a heavy-based saucepan. Whisking constantly, add the polenta in a thin stream and stir until it thickens and starts to come away from the side of the pan. Remove from the heat, add the parmesan and butter, season with sea salt and freshly ground black pepper and stir until the cheese and butter have melted.

Pour into a lightly greased 22 cm (8½ inch) square baking tin and smooth the surface. Allow to cool to room temperature, then refrigerate for 2 hours, or until firm. Turn the polenta out onto a chopping board, trim the edges and cut into four even squares.

While the polenta is cooling, make the anchovy sauce. Combine the anchovies and rosemary in a food processor and blend until a paste forms. With the motor running, add the olive oil in a thin stream, then add the lemon juice and season with sea salt and freshly ground black pepper.

Preheat a barbecue chargrill plate to medium. Grill the polenta squares for 7–8 minutes on each side, or until crisp and golden, then move them to the side of the grill. Season the lamb with sea salt and cook for 2–3 minutes on each side for medium–rare, or until done to your liking. Transfer to a warmed plate, cover loosely with foil and leave to rest in a warm place for 5 minutes.

To serve, slice the lamb fillets into four pieces on the diagonal, cutting across the grain. Put the grilled polenta on warmed serving plates, top with the lamb and rocket leaves and drizzle with the anchovy sauce.

Abbacchio (Roman lamb)

Serves 4–6

ROSEMARY POTATOES

125 ml (4 fl oz/½ cup) extra virgin olive oil
2 rosemary sprigs, each about 12 cm (4½ inches) long
8 garlic cloves, unpeeled
1.5 kg (3 lb 5 oz) roasting potatoes, peeled and cut into 4 cm (1½ inch) cubes

3 tablespoons olive oil
1 kg (2 lb 4 oz) shoulder of spring lamb, bone in, cut into 2 cm (¾ inch) pieces (ask your butcher to do this)
2 garlic cloves, crushed
6 sage leaves
1 rosemary sprig
1 tablespoon plain (all-purpose) flour
125 ml (4 fl oz/½ cup) white wine vinegar
6 anchovy fillets

Preheat the oven to 180°C (350°F/Gas 4). To make the rosemary potatoes, pour the olive oil into a large baking tin, add the rosemary, garlic and potato and toss to coat. Transfer to the middle shelf of the oven and bake for 30 minutes. Turn the potatoes, sprinkle with sea salt and bake for a further 30 minutes, or until crisp and golden.

Meanwhile, heat the olive oil in a heavy-based frying pan with a lid. Add the lamb and cook in batches over medium heat for 3–4 minutes, turning to brown all over.

Return all the lamb to the pan and add the garlic, sage and rosemary. Season with sea salt and freshly ground black pepper, stir well and cook for 1 minute.

Using a small, fine sieve, dust the lamb with the flour, then cook for a further 1 minute. Add the vinegar, simmer for 30 seconds, then add 250 ml (9 fl oz/1 cup) water. Cook, partially covered, over low heat for 50–60 minutes, or until the lamb is tender, adding a little more water if needed.

When the lamb is almost cooked, mash the anchovies to a paste with 1 tablespoon of the cooking liquid using a mortar and pestle. Add to the lamb and cook, uncovered, for a further 2 minutes. Serve immediately, with the rosemary potatoes.

Middle eastern lamb and pine nut pizzas

Makes 6

1 ½ teaspoons dried yeast
½ teaspoon caster (superfine) sugar
450 g (1 lb/3⅔ cups) strong white flour
1 teaspoon salt
1 tablespoon olive oil
lemon wedges, to serve
Greek-style yoghurt, to serve

TOPPING
2 tablespoons olive oil
1 small onion, finely chopped
1 garlic clove, finely chopped
250 g (9 oz) minced (ground) lamb
400 g (14 oz) tin whole tomatoes, drained and chopped
3 tablespoons pine nuts, toasted
¼ teaspoon ground allspice
¼ teaspoon ground cinnamon
1 tablespoon lemon juice

Put 3 tablespoons warm water in a small bowl. Sprinkle the yeast and sugar over, stir to dissolve the sugar, then leave in a draught-free place for 10 minutes, or until the yeast is foamy.

Put the flour and salt in the bowl of an electric mixer with a dough hook attachment and make a well in the centre. Pour the yeast mixture into the well, then, with the mixer set to its lowest speed, gradually add 250 ml (9 fl oz/1 cup) water and the olive oil. Mix for 3 minutes, or until a dough forms. Increase the speed to medium and knead for a further 10 minutes, or until the dough is smooth and elastic. (Alternatively, mix the dough by hand using a wooden spoon, then turn out onto a floured work surface and knead for 10 minutes, or until the dough is smooth and elastic.)

Transfer the dough to a large oiled bowl, turning the dough to coat in the oil. Cover with plastic wrap and leave to rise in a draught-free place for 1 ½–2 hours, or until doubled in size.

Meanwhile, prepare the topping. Heat the olive oil in a frying pan over medium heat. Add the onion and sauté for 5 minutes, or until softened, then add the garlic and lamb and sauté for 5 minutes, turning to brown all over. Add the tomatoes, pine nuts, spices and lemon juice and season to taste with sea salt and freshly ground black pepper. Remove from the heat and leave to cool.

Preheat the oven to 220°C (425°F/Gas 7) and grease three baking trays. Knock back the dough by punching it gently, then turn out onto a floured work surface. Divide the dough into six equal portions and shape into balls, then roll out until 5 mm (¼ inch) thick. Transfer to the baking trays. Divide the topping among the pizza bases, leaving a 1 cm (½ inch) border around the edges.

Bake the pizzas, one tray at a time, for 10–12 minutes, or until the edges are golden and the base is crisp. Serve hot with lemon wedges and yoghurt.

Lamb crown roast with sage stuffing

Serves 4–6

- 1 crown roast of lamb, with 12 cutlets
- 20 g (3/4 oz) butter
- 2 onions, chopped
- 1 green apple, peeled and chopped
- 160 g (5 1/2 oz/2 cups) fresh breadcrumbs
- 2 tablespoons chopped sage
- 1 tablespoon chopped flat-leaf (Italian) parsley
- 3 tablespoons unsweetened apple juice
- 2 eggs, separated

Preheat the oven to 210°C (415°F/Gas 6–7). Trim the lamb of excess fat and sinew.

Melt the butter in a saucepan. Add the onion and apple and sauté over medium heat for 5 minutes, or until the onion has softened. Tip into a bowl, add the breadcrumbs, sage and parsley and mix well. Whisk together the apple juice and egg yolks, then stir into the breadcrumb mixture.

Using electric beaters, whisk the egg whites until soft peaks form, then fold into the stuffing mixture.

Place the roast on a sheet of greased foil in a roasting tin. Wrap some foil around the tops of the bones to stop them burning. Spoon the stuffing into the cavity, then roast the lamb for 45 minutes for medium–rare, or until cooked to your liking.

Remove from the oven, cover loosely with foil and leave to rest in a warm place for 10 minutes before serving.

Lamb pilaff

Serves 4

1 large eggplant (aubergine), cut into 1 cm (½ inch) cubes
125 ml (4 fl oz/½ cup) olive oil
1 large onion, finely chopped
½ teaspoon ground cinnamon
1 teaspoon ground cumin
½ teaspoon ground coriander
300 g (10½ oz/1½ cups) long-grain white rice
500 ml (17 fl oz/2 cups) chicken or vegetable stock
2 tomatoes, cut into wedges
3 tablespoons toasted pistachios
2 tablespoons currants
2 tablespoons chopped coriander (cilantro)

MEATBALLS
500 g (1 lb 2 oz) minced (ground) lamb
½ teaspoon ground allspice
½ teaspoon ground cinnamon
1 teaspoon ground cumin
½ teaspoon ground coriander
2 tablespoons olive oil

Put the eggplant in a colander, sprinkle with salt and leave for 1 hour. Rinse, drain well, then pat dry with paper towels.

Heat 2 tablespoons of the olive oil in a large, deep, frying pan, add the eggplant and cook over medium heat for 10 minutes. Remove and drain on paper towels.

Heat the remaining olive oil in the pan, add the onion and sauté for 5 minutes, or until softened. Stir in the ground spices, then add the rice and stir to coat. Pour in the stock, season with sea salt and freshly ground black pepper and bring to the boil. Reduce the heat and simmer, covered, for 15 minutes.

Meanwhile, make the meatballs. Put the lamb in a bowl with the ground spices. Season with sea salt and freshly ground black pepper and mix well. Roll the mixture into small balls the size of walnuts.

Heat the olive oil in a frying pan and cook the meatballs in batches over medium heat for 5 minutes, turning often to brown all over. Drain on paper towels.

Add the tomato wedges to the frying pan and cook for 3–5 minutes, or until softened.

Stir the eggplant, pistachios, currants and meatballs through the rice. Serve the pilaff with the tomato wedges, sprinkled with the coriander.

Lamb fillets wrapped in vine leaves with avgolemono sauce

Serves 4

12 lamb loin fillets (about 700 g/1 lb 9 oz in total), trimmed
2 teaspoons lemon juice
3 garlic cloves, crushed
½ teaspoon ground allspice
2 tablespoons olive oil
1 kg (2 lb 4 oz) unpeeled boiling potatoes, such as pink fir apple or kipfler (fingerling)
12 large vine leaves, preserved in brine

AVGOLEMONO SAUCE
2 eggs
1 egg yolk
3 tablespoons lemon juice
100 ml (3½ fl oz) chicken stock

Put the lamb fillets in a bowl with the lemon juice, garlic, allspice and half the olive oil. Mix to coat, then cover and set aside for 1 hour.

Meanwhile, steam or boil the potatoes for 10–15 minutes, or until just tender. When cool enough to handle, peel the potatoes and slice each one in half lengthways. Gently toss in a bowl with the remaining olive oil and season with sea salt and freshly ground black pepper.

Rinse the vine leaves in warm water, drain well, then pat dry with paper towels. Remove any woody stems.

Remove the lamb from the marinade and drain well. Lay the vine leaves flat, vein side up, then place a lamb fillet along the base of each leaf. Season the lamb well, then roll up each leaf to enclose the lamb, with the seam underneath.

To make the avgolemono sauce, put the eggs, egg yolk and lemon juice in a bowl and whisk together well. In a small saucepan, bring the stock to the boil. Add 1 tablespoon of the hot stock to the egg mixture, whisk to combine, then slowly add the egg mixture to the stock over low heat, stirring continuously. Cook over low heat, stirring constantly with a wooden spoon, for 4–5 minutes, or until the sauce thickens enough to coat the back of the spoon. Do not let it boil or it will curdle. Cover and keep in a warm place — but not over direct heat or the sauce will curdle.

Meanwhile, preheat a barbecue chargrill plate or chargrill pan to medium. Chargrill the potatoes for 6–7 minutes, or until golden and crisp. Remove and keep warm. Chargrill the lamb parcels for 1–2 minutes on each side for medium–rare, or until cooked to your liking.

Slice the lamb parcels in half on the diagonal. Serve with the potatoes and the warm avgolemono sauce.

pork

With the exception of Muslim countries and Israel, pork is eaten pretty much the globe over. It is overwhelmingly the meat of preference throughout Asia and many parts of Europe. China is thought to consume about a third of the world's pork, with each of its 1.2 billion citizens (give or take) consuming nearly 1 kg (2 lb 4 oz) of pork products every 10 days — but astonishingly, Austrians, Germans and Danish consume slightly more than this.

The pig occurs widely on every continent except Antarctica. European prehistoric cave-art representations of pigs, such as those at Lascaux, indicate its importance even to our hunter-gatherer ancestors. Descended from the Asiatic wild boar, the pig was probably first domesticated in China or the Near East around 5000 B.C.E., and in Europe around 1500 B.C.E. In China, the very first pictogram for 'home' depicted a pig under a roof, and the modern, generic Chinese word for 'pork' is the same as that for 'meat'.

The pig was the main source of meat for ancient Athenians and was also wildly popular in Rome. The Romans formulated laws governing the butchery of pork and perfected techniques for preserving it by smoking and salting. Apicius, the ancient Roman cookbook author, wrote copious pork recipes, pairing it variously with honey, sweet wine and cumin.

Easy to raise as it doesn't require a lot of space, and a legendarily non-fussy eater (pigs are omnivorous, partial to mushrooms, bulbs, tubers, fruits, worms, snails, small rodents, eggs and small birds), the pig has always been a highly valued food source, particularly among the poor. The annual slaughter of pigs (traditionally after fattening over summer) has long been associated with festivities and merry-making. The Roman satirist Juvenal described the pig as 'the animal born for feasting', so important was its place at the Roman banquet table, and indeed in centuries since.

Modern pork

The modern pig is virtually unrecognisable from several centuries ago and has morphed from two distinct types: the European and Chinese pig. The former were scrawny and long-legged, the latter squat and plump. Most meat pigs today are long-bodied for maximum meat, lean and have extra-long loins, which is the most valuable part. Among the most popular breeds for industrialised farming are the Large White, the Duroc and Landrace.

Conventional versus free range

While lean pork has its benefits, some fat tastes great — and pigs without enough of it don't. Modern, mass-produced pork is pale in colour, low in fat and insipid in flavour. Like so many of our other meats, pork is raised in high-density situations where diet is rigidly controlled and 'undesirable' traits are bred out. Pigs raised in these conditions also suffer the indignity of tail docking and teeth-filing (through boredom, these gregarious, intelligent animals fight and tails get bitten). It is a pity that the consumer-led demand for lean pork has produced some very unhappy pigs and pretty boring pork.

Generally, today's pork lacks the character and sweet 'piggyness' of 'real' pork, which is produced when pigs, which are natural foragers, rooters and roamers, are allowed space to wander, are fed a varied diet, and given time to accumulate layers of flavour-providing fat. The aim of pork production today is to produce the greatest quantity of meat in the shortest possible time and in the cheapest possible way.

Pork that has free-ranged and had a varied diet produces meat that is quite deep pink in colour, and some cuts will exhibit marbling in the flesh. The flavour is incomparable. A growing number of farmers, mainly following organic, free-range practices, as well as those fighting to keep alive 'heritage' breeds of pig — such as the Berkshire, Saddleback, Tamworth and Large Black — are producing wonderful, flavoursome pork. You may have to search to find it, and pay significantly more for it, but this is pork (and ham and bacon) that is worth buying and cooking.

The sweetest, best-tasting pork has traditionally come from the female, or sow. The meat of males (boars) has a hard texture and an unpleasant odour called 'boar taint', caused by a sex steroid. These days, male pigs are castrated and slaughtered so young that boar taint is no longer an issue.

However, good butchers (and those in Asian enclaves) still supply only sow meat to their customers — always be sure to ask. Incidentally, Asian cooks also prefer a decent amount of fat on their pork — another reason to shop at Chinese or Vietnamese butchers if you can — although their cuts will be rather different to those you may be used to.

Buying and storing pork

Pork doesn't have the tough connective tissues of beef so it doesn't require aging; also, the unsaturated fats in pork go rancid quite quickly.

As a general rule, avoid very pale meat. Very pale pork indicates possible low pH levels, which makes for tough, stringy, watery meat. It should be a robust pink to pinkish-red in colour, and look dry with firmish, white fat. Avoid pork that looks grey or has yellowing fat or tacky-looking meat. These traits signify lack of freshness.

Replace any wrapping with fresh plastic wrap and use fresh pork within 2 days of purchase, and minced (ground) pork within a day. Make sure the meat isn't sitting in bloody juices. To freeze pork, wrap it well in several layers of plastic to protect against freezer burn and freeze for up to 3 months. Store leftover cooked pork away from any uncooked meats in the refrigerator, well wrapped, and use it within 3 days.

Nutritional content

Pork is higher in B vitamins than any other meat. It is rich in zinc, potassium and phosphorous and a good source of iron. Despite being called 'the other white meat', pork is in fact a red meat.

There is even something to be said for the health-giving properties of pork fat (lard), which was once widely used in cooking for the special flavour and texture it imparts. In her book *Delicioso*, food writer Penelope Casas says lard has been found to 'have many of the healthful qualities of olive oil; it is much lower in saturated fats than butter or beef fats and has the acids that seem to … reduce cholesterol levels'. While large intakes of any fat source are unhealthy, it is interesting to note how traditional diets made good nutritional sense.

Naturally rendered lard is better than the lard sold in supermarkets, which has been made using chemical processes such as bleaching, filtering and hydrogenating. It is easy to render lard. Buy some pork back fat from your butcher and cut it into 2.5 cm (1 inch) pieces. Place in a large, heavy-based pan, then add enough water to cover the base of the pan. Cook over a very low heat for 4–5 hours, stirring often, until the fat has all melted and is clear. Strain the lard through several layers of muslin (cheesecloth), then cool and cover tightly. Any golden solids strained out are delicious tossed through simple leafy salads or tossed into soup as a garnish. The solid lard can be kept in the refrigerator for up to 2 months, or frozen for up to 3 months.

Pork cuts

A pig is best thought of as three parts: the shoulder, neck and foreleg region; the loin and belly region; and the ham or rear leg section.

The shoulder yields the spare rib roast (used on or off the bone), shoulder roast and picnic ham. In North America the cuts from this part of the pig are called the Boston roast and the picnic shoulder roast. Some countries value the neck as a cut (it makes a rich and juicy pot-roast), and also the 'hand', which is cut from both the forward part of the belly and the upper foreleg. The shank, hock, trotter and head are lesser cuts from the shoulder, but much valued in many parts of the world.

The loin, or back area, yields the rack of pork, loin roast, loin and chump chops, tenderloin, eye of loin, blade and sirloin — names and cuts vary from country to country. The belly is often sold as rolled belly, or as the thick or thin end of belly; spare ribs also originate from here. The belly, which has alternating layers of meat and visible fat, can be roasted, braised or cut into strips and grilled, and is a particularly succulent part of the pig.

The ham or leg gives whole leg roasts (or hams, if processed), another set of trotters, and also the tail, which some cooks use.

COOKING PORK

In days gone by, pork had to be thoroughly cooked through to be safely edible, as the meat harboured worms causing a parasitic disease called trichinosis. So pork was always cooked very well indeed — and the habit persists. These days, however, trichinosis is rare in developed countries. Trichinosis worms are destroyed at 58°C (137°F), so it is not necessary to overcook pork — in fact, grilled or roasted cuts are best a little pink in the middle. This is especially true of leaner pork: cook it all the way through and it will be dry and wholly without character, particularly the ultra-lean pieces such as tenderloin (eye fillet), loin roasts and loin chops.

Pork is a most versatile meat. It forms the basis of the beloved sausage, as well as the rich and varied French *charcuterie* (or cooked meat) dishes, pâtés, terrines, rillettes, galantines and jellied savoury preparations. Pasta sauces, quick grills, flash fries, unctuous braises and hefty, juicy roasts starring pork abound, complemented by all manner of flavours, ingredients and accompaniments. Those that are slightly acidic help to cut pork's sweet fattiness; sweet foods such as apple sauce, pineapple, orange, prunes, honey and maple syrup are legendary for their affinity with pork — as are strong, tart ingredients such as sauerkraut, capers, cornichons and mustard, and herbs like sage and rosemary. Asian ingredients (ginger, soy, fish sauce and dried spices like star anise) also team brilliantly with pork.

Roasting

There is something extremely celebratory about a large pork roast, complete with apple sauce or sauerkraut and the all-important crisp crackling. The most important thing is not to overcook a pork roast — it can stand to be a little pink in the middle. (Roasting to an internal temperature of 58°C/137°F will destroy trichinosis worms, at which stage the pork will still be pink and juicy.) For thoroughly cooked pork, a final internal temperature of 70°C (158°F) will do, but as it needs to rest after cooking, remove it from the oven at 60°C (140°F), as the internal temperature will keep rising for some time.

Fattier cuts can be roasted to an even higher internal temperature (up to 68°C/155°F) as their fat will keep them thoroughly moist. Very lean, tender cuts — such as tenderloin (eye fillet), loin roasts and loin chops — should be roasted to no higher than 70°C (158°F). Sear larger cuts in a very hot oven (220°C/425°F/Gas 7) for 30 minutes first to seal their exterior, then reduce the temperature to 180°C (350°F/Gas 4) to complete the cooking.

Many pork cuts are suited to roasting, including any of the shoulder roasts, the neck, the loin, the whole leg and the belly.

Making crackling

Crisp, golden and chewy, a layer of crackling on a succulent pork roast is as much anticipated as the meat itself. To achieve perfect crackling, first score the skin at regular intervals with a very sharp knife — this stops the skin shrinking and deforming the roast during cooking, and also makes the finished crackling easier to cut or break into pieces. Rub the skin all over with a little olive oil and sea salt, then roast for 20–30 minutes at 200°C (400°F/Gas 6). Reduce the heat to 180°C (350°F/Gas 4) and cook until the meat is done, basting the crackling occasionally with the fat from the roasting tin (avoid the meat juices as these will moisten the crackling). The crackling will lift off easily after cooking, although if your roast is a large one, it may be necessary to cut it into two pieces to do this.

Sausages

Among the first records of sausages are those of the Chinese *lapcheong* from as early as 3000 B.C.E., and blood sausage, which Homer mentioned in *The Odyssey*. Arguably it is pork that goes into the world's most famed and fine sausages. Basically, sausages comprise a coarse 'paste' of minced (ground) meat, fat and flavourings, which are extruded into a thin casing and sealed with a twist or a knot. Sausages can be fresh, smoked or otherwise preserved. The word for sausage derives from the French word *saucisse*, 'to preserve with salt'. Salt in sausages provides seasoning, has an antibacterial function and helps the filling bind together.

Long thought of as a poor man's food, sausage-making is the outcome of efficient butchery, where nothing (including scraps, off-cuts and organ meats) is wasted. These days, all sorts of fillers, fats and marginal 'meat' ends up in fresh commercial sausages. The original casings for sausages were animal intestines, but artificial ones (made of cellulose, collagen or even plastic!) are more the norm today. In the United Kingdom, cereal fillers can account for up to 25% of the ingredients in fresh sausages; the real, lean meat content of a sausage can be under 30%. It is also likely they'll contain polyphosphates (to retain water), soya (for bulk), sulphates (for shelf-life), antioxidants (to enhance flavour), colour and preservatives. Elsewhere in Europe, most traditional sausages still comprise 100% meat and fat, and in the United States, the use of fillers and extenders is largely banned.

Of course, not all commercial sausage-makers are scurrilous cheapskates. There has been a movement back towards 'real' sausages at the boutique end of the market and this is a good thing. Customers might resist paying a premium for a humble sausage, but a well-crafted product, made from the highest-quality ingredients, is worth every cent.

Fresh sausages should be used within two days. They are best when fried, grilled or roasted; some cooks prick them a few times first and blanch them in gently simmering water to speed the cooking process and ensure they are cooked properly in the middle. Don't cook sausages over too high a heat or the meat inside will toughen (you'll lose their silky texture) and they could spurt hot fat or liquid, losing flavour and moistness.

Braising and poaching

Certain cuts of pork are delicious in stews, braises and pot roasts, but not very lean ones, which will become cardboard-like if subjected to long, slow, moist methods of cooking. Pork flesh does not contain great quantities of collagen, a connective tissue that breaks down and softens during long, slow cooking; instead, it contains more of a connective tissue called elastin, which doesn't soften during cooking but rather shrinks and hardens.

The best parts for braising are the belly (which is quite fatty, and so is not to everyone's taste), ribs and shoulder. Pork neck can also be braised as it contains quite a lot of fat. The shanks, sometimes cut across the bone into pieces similar to veal osso bucco, can also be treated this way; as with all meat, pork on the bone always has more flavour.

When braising pork, often quite sweet and/or strong flavours are employed: honey, maple syrup, rosemary, sage, spices (cinnamon, star anise, fennel seed), orange juice, prunes and apples are all good. The pork is first browned before adding the other ingredients and simmering. Because of its inherent tenderness, it won't take as long as other red meats to cook.

Trotters and hocks are best gently poached in plenty of just-simmering stock or water. Sometimes, trotters cooked this way are then cooked again by a second method — the French crumb the well-drained trotters, then grill them. The French (and Chinese too) also poach the ears in stock, water or court-bouillon (water flavoured with aromatics and vegetables), then cut them into strips and toss through a salad, or press and jelly them, or crumb and then grill them.

Frying and grilling

Tender meat and decent amounts of lubricating fat are the perfect combination for this style of cooking — throw in a bone or two and the flavour is even better. Loin chops, chump chops, pieces of tenderloin (eye fillet), escalopes cut from the loin, spareribs or diced pieces of leg or shoulder all make for admirable grills or barbecues.

While pork should be served juicily pink, like veal you'd never serve it rare, so the longer cooking time it requires also means you need to cook it over a slightly lower heat than you might for, say, beef.

Always trim the excess fat from pork before grilling as this can 'flare' or burn while cooking — but do leave at least a thin layer on cutlets and the like. Pork should be well brushed with oil before grilling; very lean cuts will need basting with oil (or marinating before cooking and brushing with the marinade) while on the heat.

Sear the meat well over quite high heat for a minute on each side, then cook on a lower heat (or further away from the heat source if barbecuing) until done. The cooking time depends entirely upon how thick the meat is and whether it is on or off the bone. For best results, have chops, cutlets and steaks cut to 1–1.5 cm (1/2–5/8 inch) thickness.

Tender, lean chunks of pork steak, cutlet off-the-bone or tenderloin (eye fillet), cut to an equal size, are ideal for grilling on skewers. Brush them well with oil and grill as above.

As a guide, the internal temperature of grilled pork should register 62°C (145°F) when cooked. Be sure to cover the meat loosely with foil and rest it in a warm place for 3–5 minutes before serving.

Italian meatballs with tomato sauce

Serves 4

MEATBALLS

185 ml (6 fl oz/$^{3}/_{4}$ cup) olive oil
1 onion, finely chopped
75 g (2$^{1}/_{2}$ oz/$^{1}/_{2}$ cup) pine nuts, roughly chopped
3 garlic cloves, crushed
2 large handfuls of parsley, roughly chopped
3 tablespoons roughly chopped basil or rosemary
2 teaspoons fennel seeds, ground
50 g (1$^{3}/_{4}$ oz/$^{2}/_{3}$ cup) fresh breadcrumbs
250 g (9 oz/1 cup) ricotta cheese
3 tablespoons grated parmesan cheese
grated zest of 1 large lemon
1 egg
500 g (1 lb 2 oz) minced (ground) pork

TOMATO SAUCE

800 g (1 lb 12 oz) ripe, firm tomatoes, or 2 x 400 g (14 oz) tins chopped tomatoes
100 ml (3$^{1}/_{2}$ fl oz) red wine

Start by making the meatballs. Heat half the olive oil in a frying pan. Add the onion and pine nuts and sauté for 5–6 minutes, or until the onion has softened and the pine nuts are light golden. Add the garlic and cook for a few minutes more, then set aside to cool.

Combine the remaining meatball ingredients in a bowl. Add the cooled onion mixture, season with sea salt and freshly ground black pepper and mix until well combined. Fry a piece of the mixture to check the seasoning, and adjust if necessary. Refrigerate for at least 30 minutes or overnight to allow the flavours to develop.

When you're ready to cook, roll the meatball mixture into walnut-sized balls.

Heat the remaining olive oil in a large frying pan. Add the meatballs in batches and cook for 8 minutes, or until golden brown all over, turning them now and then and ensuring there is enough oil to prevent the meatballs sticking to the pan. Remove and set aside while making the sauce.

If using fresh tomatoes, score a cross in the base of each tomato using a small, sharp knife. Plunge the tomatoes into boiling water for 20 seconds, then remove and plunge into iced water to cool. Peel the skin away from the cross and finely chop the flesh.

Put the tomatoes and wine in a large saucepan, season with sea salt and freshly ground black pepper and simmer for 5 minutes. Carefully add the meatballs to the sauce. Reduce the heat to a gentle simmer, then cover and cook for a further 10 minutes. Allow to stand for 10 minutes before serving.

Pork noisettes with prunes

Serves 4

16 prunes, pitted
1 tablespoon olive oil
60 g (2 1/4 oz) butter
8 pork noisettes (medallions), trimmed of all fat and membranes (see Note)
1 onion, finely chopped
125 ml (4 fl oz/1/2 cup) white wine
310 ml (10 3/4 fl oz/1 1/4 cups) chicken or veal stock
1 bay leaf
2 thyme sprigs
250 ml (9 fl oz/1 cup) thick (double/heavy) cream

Put the prunes in a small saucepan, cover with cold water and bring to the boil. Reduce the heat and simmer for 5 minutes. Drain well and set aside.

Heat the olive oil in a large heavy-based frying pan and add half the butter. When the butter starts foaming, add the pork, in batches if necessary, and cook over medium–high heat for 4–5 minutes, or until cooked but still slightly pink in the middle, turning once. Transfer the pork to a warm plate, cover loosely with foil and leave to rest in a warm place.

Pour off any excess fat from the frying pan. Melt the remaining butter in the pan, add the onion and sauté over low heat for 5 minutes, or until softened but not browned. Add the wine, bring to the boil and simmer for 2 minutes, then add the stock, bay leaf and thyme sprigs and bring to the boil. Reduce the heat and simmer for 10 minutes, or until the mixture has reduced by half.

Strain the stock mixture into a bowl, discarding the solids. Rinse the frying pan and place back over low heat. Add the stock, cream and prunes and simmer for 8 minutes, or until the sauce thickens slightly. Return the pork to the pan, simmer until heated through and serve.

NOTE: You can also use two 375 g (13 oz) pork fillets for this recipe. Trim them, then cut each on the diagonal into four even-sized pieces, reserving any off-cuts for another use.

Adobo pork with coconut rice

Serves 6

170 ml ($5\frac{1}{2}$ fl oz/$\frac{2}{3}$ cup) balsamic vinegar
4 tablespoons soy sauce
3 bay leaves
4 garlic cloves, crushed
$\frac{1}{2}$ teaspoon freshly ground black pepper
6 pork loin chops
2 tablespoons peanut oil
lime wedges, to serve

COCONUT RICE
400 g (14 oz/2 cups) jasmine rice
2 tablespoons peanut oil
1 small onion, finely diced
1 teaspoon grated fresh ginger
2 garlic cloves, crushed
625 ml ($21\frac{1}{2}$ fl oz/$2\frac{1}{2}$ cups) coconut milk

Put the vinegar, soy sauce, bay leaves, garlic and pepper in a large non-metallic dish and mix well. Add the pork chops and turn to coat, then cover and refrigerate for at least 3 hours, or preferably overnight.

To make the coconut rice, rinse the rice under cold, running water until the water runs clear, then drain well. Heat the peanut oil in a heavy-based saucepan over medium heat, then add the onion, ginger and garlic. Sauté for 3 minutes, or until the onion has softened, then add the rice and stir until the rice is coated in oil.

Stir in the coconut milk, bring to the boil, then turn the heat down as low as possible. Cover and cook for 15 minutes, then remove from the heat and let the rice sit, covered, for 5 minutes. Gently fluff the rice with a fork and season well with sea salt and freshly ground black pepper.

Meanwhile, preheat a barbecue chargrill plate or chargrill pan to medium. Remove the pork from the marinade, draining well, and pat dry with paper towels. Brush the pork with the peanut oil, season with sea salt and freshly ground black pepper and cook for 6–8 minutes on each side, or until just cooked through — the pork should still be a little pink in the middle. Remove from the heat, cover loosely with foil and leave to rest in a warm place for 3–5 minutes.

Serve with the coconut rice and lime wedges.

NOTE: Grilled mango cheeks are delicious with this dish. Cut the cheeks off 3 small mangoes, down either side of the stone, then score the flesh using a sharp knife, without cutting through the skin. Lightly brush the cut surface with 2 teaspoons oil, then place on a barbecue chargrill plate or a chargrill pan, skin side down, and cook over medium heat for 2 minutes. Turn the mango cheeks 90° and grill for a further 2 minutes to pattern the mango with crossed grill marks. Serve warm.

Pork chops with braised red cabbage

Serves 4

BRAISED RED CABBAGE
2 tablespoons clarified butter
1 onion, finely chopped
1 garlic clove, crushed
1 small red cabbage, shredded
1 apple, peeled, cored and finely sliced
4 tablespoons red wine
1 tablespoon red wine vinegar
1/4 teaspoon ground cloves
1 tablespoon finely chopped sage

1 tablespoon clarified butter
4 x 175 g (6 oz) pork chops, trimmed
4 tablespoons white wine
420 ml (14 1/2 fl oz/1 2/3 cups) chicken stock
3 tablespoons thick (double/heavy) cream
1 1/2 tablespoons dijon mustard
4 sage leaves

To make the braised cabbage, heat the butter in a large saucepan, add the onion and garlic and sauté over medium heat for 6–7 minutes, or until the onion has softened. Add the remaining ingredients and season with sea salt and freshly ground black pepper. Cover and cook for 30 minutes over very low heat. Remove the lid and stir over medium–high heat for 5 minutes to evaporate any liquid.

Meanwhile, begin preparing the pork. Heat the butter in a frying pan, add the pork chops and brown over medium–high heat for 2 minutes on each side. Season to taste with sea salt and freshly ground black pepper. Pour in the wine and stock, then cover and simmer for 15–20 minutes, or until tender.

Remove the pork to a warmed plate, cover loosely with foil and leave to rest while finishing the sauce.

Strain the liquid from the frying pan, then return it to the frying pan. Bring to the boil and cook until reduced by two-thirds. Add the cream and mustard and stir over very low heat until the sauce has thickened slightly; do not allow the cream to come to the boil.

Place the pork on warmed serving plates, drizzle generously with the sauce and garnish with a sage leaf. Serve with the braised red cabbage.

Pasta, bean and sausage soup

Serves 4

4 tablespoons olive oil
90 g (3¼ oz) piece of pancetta, finely chopped
1 onion, finely chopped
2 garlic cloves, finely chopped
1 celery stalk, finely chopped
1 carrot, finely chopped
1 bay leaf
400 g (14 oz) tin chopped tomatoes, drained
1.6 litres (55½ fl oz/6½ cups) chicken stock
200 g (7 oz/1 cup) dried borlotti (cranberry) beans, soaked overnight and drained
5 good-quality Italian-style fresh pork sausages
150 g (5½ oz) ditalini or other small dried pasta
2 tablespoons chopped oregano
extra virgin olive oil, to serve
grated parmesan cheese, to serve

Heat 3 tablespoons of the olive oil in a large saucepan. Add the pancetta, onion, garlic, celery and carrot and sauté over medium heat for 7–8 minutes, or until the onion is golden.

Add the bay leaf, tomatoes, stock and beans and bring to the boil. Reduce the heat and simmer for 1½ hours, or until the beans are tender. Discard the bay leaf.

Transfer 250 ml (9 fl oz/1 cup) of the soup mixture to a food processor, blend until smooth, then stir back into the soup.

Remove the casings from the sausages and roughly crumble the meat. Heat the remaining olive oil in a frying pan, add the sausage meat and cook for 8 minutes, or until golden, stirring to break up any lumps. Using a slotted spoon, remove the sausage meat and add it to the soup, along with the pasta.

Cover and simmer for 6–8 minutes, or until the pasta is *al dente*. Stir in the oregano, then divide the soup among four warmed bowls. Drizzle each with olive oil, scatter with parmesan and serve.

Warm pork salad with blue cheese croutons

Serves 4

1 small or ½ large baguette
125 ml (4 fl oz/½ cup) olive oil
1 large garlic clove, crushed
400 g (14 oz) pork fillet, cut into 5 mm (¼ inch) slices
100 g (3½ oz) blue cheese, crumbled
2 tablespoons sherry vinegar
½ teaspoon soft brown sugar
150 g (5½ oz) mixed salad leaves

Preheat the grill (broiler) to high. Cut the baguette into 20 slices, each about 5 mm (¼ inch) thick.

Put the olive oil and garlic in a screw-top jar and shake to mix well. Heat 2 teaspoons of the garlic oil in a frying pan, add half the pork slices and cook over medium–high heat for 1 minute on each side. Remove and keep warm. Add another 2 teaspoons of the garlic oil to the frying pan and cook the remaining pork slices, then remove. Season all the pork with sea salt and freshly ground black pepper and keep warm.

Spread the bread slices on a baking tray and brush on one side with a little of the remaining garlic oil. Toast under the hot grill until golden. Turn the bread over, sprinkle with the crumbled cheese, then return to the grill and cook until the cheese has melted (this will happen very quickly).

Add the vinegar and sugar to the remaining garlic oil in the jar and shake well. Place the salad leaves in a large bowl, add the pork and pour the salad dressing over. Toss well.

Divide the salad among four plates and arrange five croutons around the edge of each salad. Serve immediately.

Braised sausages with puy lentils

Serves 4

1 tablespoon olive oil
100 g (3½ oz) pancetta, cut into cubes
2 red onions, finely chopped
12 Toulouse sausages, or any good-quality fresh pork sausages
2 garlic cloves, bruised
2 thyme sprigs
300 g (10½ oz/1½ cups) puy lentils or tiny blue-green lentils
750 ml (26 fl oz/3 cups) tinned chicken consommé
150 g (5½ oz) baby English spinach leaves, finely chopped
crusty bread, to serve

Heat the olive oil in a large heavy-based frying pan. Add the pancetta and sauté over medium–high heat for 5–6 minutes, or until browned. Using a slotted spoon, remove the pancetta and place in a bowl.

Add the onion to the pan and sauté over medium heat for 5–6 minutes, or until softened and only lightly browned. Remove the onion and add to the pancetta.

Fry the sausages in the same pan, in batches if necessary, for 10 minutes, or until deep golden all over, turning often.

Return the pancetta and onion to the pan, add the garlic, thyme and lentils and stir together well. Pour in the consommé and bring to the boil. Reduce the heat, cover and simmer for 30–35 minutes, or until the lentils are tender.

Stir in the spinach and season to taste with sea salt and freshly ground black pepper. Serve in warmed bowls with crusty bread.

Honey-glazed ham with cumberland sauce

Serves 20

7 kg (15 lb 12 oz) smoked, cooked leg ham
cloves, for studding

HONEY GLAZE
125 g (4½ oz/⅔ cup) soft brown sugar
3 tablespoons honey
1 tablespoon hot English mustard

CUMBERLAND SAUCE
4 oranges
2 lemons
450 g (1 lb/1½ cups) redcurrant jelly
1 tablespoon dijon mustard
4 tablespoons red wine vinegar
500 ml (17 fl oz/2 cups) port

Preheat the oven to 180°C (350°F/Gas 4). Cut a line through the thick rind of the ham, 6 cm (2½ inches) from the shank end, so you can easily lift the rind. To remove the rind, run your thumb around the edge, under the cut rind, and carefully pull back, easing your hand between the fat and the rind. Using a sharp knife, lightly score the fat into a diamond pattern. Do not cut all the way through to the ham or the fat will fall off during cooking.

Put the honey glaze ingredients in a saucepan over low heat and stir until well combined. Using a palette knife or the back of a spoon, spread half the glaze over the ham, then press a clove into the centre of each diamond.

Sit the ham on a rack in a deep baking dish and pour in 500 ml (17 fl oz/2 cups) water. Cover the ham and dish tightly with greased foil and bake for 45 minutes. Gently warm the remaining glaze, then remove the baking dish from the oven and spread the glaze over the ham.

Increase the oven temperature to 210°C (415°F/Gas 6–7). Bake the ham, uncovered, for a further 20 minutes, or until the surface is golden and the glaze is lightly caramelised. Remove from the oven and leave to rest in a warm place for 15 minutes before carving.

While the ham is still in the oven, make the cumberland sauce. Using a zester, peel the zest from all the citrus, then place the zest in a small saucepan with 500 ml (17 fl oz/2 cups) water. Bring to the boil and cook for 5 minutes, then strain, discarding the liquid and reserving the zest.

Squeeze the juice from the oranges and lemons, then strain into a saucepan. Add the redcurrant jelly, mustard, vinegar, port and reserved citrus zest. Slowly bring to the boil, stirring to dissolve the jelly. Reduce the heat and simmer gently for 15 minutes. Season to taste with sea salt and freshly ground black pepper and allow to cool to room temperature. (This sauce is also delicious with turkey, venison, terrines or game.)

Carve the ham and serve with the cumberland sauce.

Pork and veal terrine

Serves 6–8

8–10 thin slices of rindless bacon
1 tablespoon olive oil
1 onion, chopped
2 garlic cloves, crushed
500 g (1 lb 2 oz) minced (ground) pork
500 g (1 lb 2 oz) minced (ground) veal
80 g (2¾ oz/1 cup) fresh white breadcrumbs
1 egg, beaten
3 tablespoons brandy
3 teaspoons chopped thyme
3 tablespoons chopped parsley

Preheat the oven to 180°C (350°F/Gas 4). Lightly grease a 25 x 11 cm (10 x 4¼ inch) terrine or non-stick baking tin. Line the terrine with the bacon, overlapping the slices slightly, to completely cover the base and sides of the tin, trimming and patching the bacon to fit as necessary and leaving the bacon hanging over the side of the terrine.

Heat the olive oil in a frying pan. Add the onion and garlic and sauté over medium heat for 5 minutes, or until the onion has softened. Tip into a large bowl, add the remaining ingredients and season well with sea salt and freshly ground black pepper. Fry a piece of the mixture to check the seasoning, then adjust if necessary; it should be very well seasoned.

Spoon the mixture into the lined terrine, pressing down firmly and smoothing the surface. Fold the overhanging bacon slices over the top to cover, trimming to fit if necessary, then cover the terrine with foil and place in a baking dish.

Pour enough hot water into the baking dish to come halfway up the side of the terrine. Bake for 1–1¼ hours, or until the juices run clear when the terrine is pierced with a skewer.

Remove the terrine from the baking dish and pour off the excess juices. Cover with foil, then cut a piece of heavy cardboard to fit the terrine and place it on top. Sit weights or tins of food on top of the cardboard to press the terrine, then refrigerate overnight.

Remove the weights and cardboard, turn the terrine out onto a serving plate, then cut into slices to serve.

Fennel-roasted pork belly with apple sauce

Serves 6–8

2 kg (4 lb 8 oz) piece of pork belly on the bone, cut from the thick end of the belly
olive oil, for brushing
2 teaspoons fennel seeds
a large pinch of ground cloves
1 tablespoon sea salt flakes
6 onions, cut in half

APPLE SAUCE
4 granny smith apples, peeled, cored and roughly chopped
1 tablespoon caster (superfine) sugar
2 cloves
1 cinnamon stick
1–2 teaspoons lemon juice, to taste

Preheat the oven to 200°C (400°F/Gas 6). Using a very sharp knife, score the pork skin in a series of 1 cm (½ inch) parallel lines, cutting about 5 mm (¼ inch) into the fat (ask your butcher to do this if you prefer). Rub a little olive oil all over the pork skin.

Using an electric spice grinder or a mortar and pestle, coarsely grind the fennel seeds. Place in a bowl with the cloves and sea salt, then rub the spices over the pork skin, rubbing well into the incisions.

Place the pork on a rack in a roasting tin and pour 500 ml (17 fl oz/2 cups) boiling water into the roasting tin (this will stop the dripping fat and juices burning). Arrange the onion halves around the pork, sitting them on the rack. Roast for 30 minutes, or until the surface of the pork skin is golden.

Reduce the oven temperature to 180°C (350°F/Gas 4) and roast the pork for a further 2 hours, or until the juices run clear when pierced through the thickest part, and the top is deep golden and very crisp. Remove the pork from the oven, cover loosely with foil and leave to rest for 20 minutes.

Meanwhile, make the apple sauce. Put the apples, sugar, cloves, cinnamon stick and 125 ml (4 fl oz/½ cup) water in a small saucepan. Stir to dissolve the sugar, then cover and simmer over low heat for 10 minutes, or until the apple is very soft. Discard the cloves and cinnamon. Mash the apple for a chunky sauce; for a very fine sauce, purée with a stick blender or in a food processor. Stir in lemon juice to taste.

Carve the pork, including the skin. Serve with the roasted onion halves, with the apple sauce passed separately.

ROAST PORK LOIN WITH BABY APPLES

SERVES 6

1.5 kg (3 lb 5 oz) rolled pork loin roast — ask your butcher to cut the rind off, but reserve the rind for cooking
600 ml (21 fl oz) apple juice, approximately
12 baby red apples, or 3 small ripe red apples

Preheat a kettle or covered barbecue to medium indirect heat. Tie the rind back onto the pork loin at 5 cm (2 inch) intervals using kitchen string. Sit the pork on a rack in a large roasting tin and pour 375 ml (13 fl oz/1½ cups) of the apple juice over.

Place the roasting tin on the barbecue grill, lower the lid and roast the pork for 15–20 minutes, checking occasionally that the apple juice isn't evaporating too quickly, and adding extra apple juice if necessary.

Reduce the heat to low, baste the pork with the pan juices and cook, covered, for a further 20 minutes, basting and adding more apple juice as needed.

Cut the apples in half, leaving the cores in. Add the apples to the pork and coat them with the pan juices. Baste the pork again, add more apple juice to the roasting tin if needed, then cook for a further 40 minutes, or until the juices run clear when the pork is tested with a skewer in the thickest part. Alternatively, test the pork using a meat thermometer — it will be cooked when the temperature reaches 75°C (167°F).

Remove the roasting tin from the heat. Transfer the pork and apples to a plate, cover loosely with foil and leave to rest in a warm place for 10 minutes. Meanwhile, check the pan juices — if they look a little thin, pour them into a small saucepan and simmer over medium heat until they reduce and thicken slightly. Season to taste.

Serve the pork with the roasted apples and pan juices.

Pork cooked in milk

Serves 6

2.25 kg (5 lb) piece of pork loin, on the bone — ask your butcher to chine and skin the loin (see Note)
2½ tablespoons olive oil
4 garlic cloves, cut in half lengthways
3 fresh bay leaves, bruised
1 litre (35 fl oz/4 cups) milk, warmed
juice of 1 lemon
a large pinch of ground cloves
grated zest of 2 lemons

Preheat the oven to 200°C (400°F/Gas 6). Trim the fat from the pork, leaving just a thin layer to keep it moist during cooking.

Heat the olive oil in a large roasting tin. Add the pork loin and cook over medium–high heat for 6–7 minutes, turning to brown all over. Remove the pork and pour off the excess fat from the roasting tin.

Add the garlic and bay leaves to the roasting tin and rest the pork on top. Season the pork with sea salt and freshly ground black pepper, then pour the milk and lemon juice over the pork. Sprinkle with the cloves and lemon zest, then roast for 20 minutes.

Reduce the oven temperature to 150°C (300°F/Gas 2) and roast the pork for a further 1–1¼ hours, or until the juices run clear when the pork is tested with a skewer in the thickest part. If necessary, add a little more milk every so often and baste the meat with the liquid every 30 minutes. Do not cover the pork — you want the liquid to reduce and the fat on the pork to become crisp.

Remove the pork from the oven, cover loosely with foil and leave to rest in a warm place for 10 minutes before carving. The sauce in the roasting tin will appear lumpy and curdled, but tastes delicious. If you prefer, you can strain the sauce before serving it with the meat. This dish is delicious with braised fennel or roasted vegetables.

NOTE: Chining means removing the backbone from the rack of ribs so you can carve between the ribs.

Red-cooked pork

Serves 8

1.5 kg (3 lb 5 oz) pork leg
4 spring onions (scallions), each tied in a knot
4 slices of fresh ginger, bashed with the flat side of a large knife or cleaver
200 ml (7 fl oz) dark soy sauce
4 tablespoons Chinese rice wine
1 teaspoon Chinese five-spice
50 g ($1\frac{3}{4}$ oz/$\frac{1}{4}$ cup) crushed rock sugar

Scrape the pork rind to make sure it is free of bristles. Blanch the pork in a saucepan of boiling water for 4–5 minutes.

Rinse the pork and place in a large flameproof casserole dish with 600 ml (21 fl oz) water and all the remaining ingredients. Bring to the boil, then reduce the heat and simmer, covered, for $2\frac{1}{2}$–3 hours, or until the meat is very tender and falling from the bone, turning the pork several times during cooking.

If there is too much liquid in the casserole dish, remove the pork and reduce the sauce by boiling it for 10–15 minutes.

Slice the pork and serve drizzled with the sauce.

Baked sticky pork ribs

Serves 4

- ½ small navel orange
- 125 ml (4 fl oz/½ cup) orange juice
- 1 large garlic clove
- ½ onion, chopped
- 1 teaspoon grated fresh ginger
- 100 ml (3½ fl oz) golden syrup or dark corn syrup
- 1 teaspoon worcestershire sauce
- 4 drops of Tabasco sauce
- 2 tablespoons tomato paste (concentrated purée)
- 16 pork spareribs
- 2 spring onions (scallions), green part only, shredded or finely sliced on the diagonal

Place the orange in a small saucepan, cover with water and bring to the boil. Reduce the heat and simmer for 5 minutes, or until soft. Drain well, then set aside to cool.

Cut the orange into large chunks, reserving any juice that runs out, then transfer the orange and any reserved juice to a food processor or blender. Add the garlic, onion and ginger and process for 25–30 seconds, or until finely chopped. Add the golden syrup, worcestershire sauce, Tabasco and tomato paste and blend until smooth.

Transfer the marinade to a shallow non-metallic dish, add the pork spareribs and toss to coat well. Cover and refrigerate for 4 hours, turning the ribs occasionally.

Preheat the oven to 180°C (350°F/Gas 4). Place the ribs in a single layer on a large baking tray, pour the marinade over and roast for 20 minutes. Turn the ribs to coat with the sauce, then roast for a further 25–30 minutes, or until tender. Serve hot or at room temperature, sprinkled with the spring onion.

Spice-rubbed pork kebabs with garlic sauce

Serves 4

2 teaspoons fennel seeds
2 teaspoons coriander seeds
1 tablespoon olive oil
800 g (1 lb 12 oz) pork neck fillet, trimmed and cut into 2 cm (3/4 inch) cubes
lemon wedges, to serve
warm pitta bread, to serve
green salad, to serve (optional)

GARLIC SAUCE
1 thick slice of good-quality, rustic white bread, crusts removed
4 garlic cloves, roughly chopped
1/2 teaspoon sea salt
3 tablespoons olive oil
1 1/2 tablespoons lemon juice

Toast the fennel and coriander seeds in a dry frying pan over medium–low heat for 30 seconds, or until fragrant, then finely grind them using a spice grinder or mortar and pestle. Tip the spices into a bowl, mix in the olive oil, then add the pork and toss to coat well. Cover and refrigerate for 2 hours.

Meanwhile, make the garlic sauce. Tear the bread into pieces and soak it in a bowl in enough warm water to cover for 5 minutes, then drain well and squeeze the bread dry. Crush the garlic with the sea salt using a mortar and pestle or a small food processor until a smooth paste forms. Add the bread to the garlic mixture, a little at a time, working to a smooth paste. Work in the olive oil 1 tablespoon at a time, then work in 3 tablespoons boiling water, 1 tablespoon at a time. Stir in the lemon juice — the sauce should be thick and smooth.

Thread the pork onto metal skewers and season well with sea salt and freshly ground black pepper.

Preheat a chargrill pan or a barbecue chargrill plate to medium–high. Chargrill the kebabs for 6–8 minutes, or until cooked through, turning onto each side only once. Drizzle with a little garlic sauce (it has a very strong flavour!) and put the remaining sauce in a small bowl to serve at the table. Serve with lemon wedges, pitta bread and a green salad, if desired.

veal

Veal is the meat from calves and is essentially a by-product of the dairy industry. Every year, in order for a cow to stay in milk production, she must bear a calf, and most calves are surplus to farm requirements. Not all of the female calves, and certainly none of the males, are needed to replenish milking herds, so an old tradition of using their meat has evolved.

The word 'veal' comes from the Roman word for calf, *vitellus*. Such was the Roman appetite for tender, young animals that emperor Alexander Severus had to forbid the slaughter of suckling animals because herds were at risk of dying out. Veal was — and still is — a luxury meat: common folk couldn't hope to eat valuable cattle until their milking and working lives were over.

To this day, because it is expensive and quite difficult to obtain (much of it goes to the restaurant trade), veal is nowhere near as widely eaten as other meats. Americans don't even consume 500 g (1 lb) of veal per person each year. Figures are much higher in Europe; Italians, for example, eat over 7 kg (15 lb) of veal each every year.

How veal is produced

Of all the food-providing animals, perhaps none attract as much sentimentality as a cute, doe-eyed calf, yet most calves have a slaughter age similar to that of pigs and lambs. Many consumers have questioned the morality of certain methods of veal production — particularly of the prized 'white' veal. Most calves reared for veal are Holstein–Friesians, and being dairy cattle, make for poor eating beyond a certain age. Calf meat is extremely pale and tender until the animal starts feeding seriously on grass at two or three months of age. When solids are introduced into their diets, the meat darkens, and with increased movement and muscle development, it also toughens.

To produce truly pale veal, weaning is delayed indefinitely and the calves are slaughtered at 4–5 months. Traditionally, muscle development has been minimised by penning the calves in tiny, individual crates or hutches, in which movement is very restricted. The calves were also kept in an anaemic state as iron in their food increases haemoglobin (red blood cell) levels in their muscle. They were instead fed an exclusively liquid, milk-based diet, causing dreadful digestive problems. Thankfully, these veal-rearing practices have been banned in most countries and there is a strong trend towards more humanely reared meat. Driven by consumer awareness and the restaurant trade, there is now a substantial niche for pinker calf meat.

Interestingly, the Italians, who consume more veal per capita than anyone else, have generally preferred their veal more pink and robustly flavoured than milk-feeding affords. This type of veal is variously called 'grain fed', 'pink' or 'rose' veal. It's important to know how such meat is produced because some die-hard aficionados still insist that the only 'real' veal is 'white' veal, so milky-hued it even smells like the stuff — a pale, tender meat with a subtle (some might say bland) flavour.

Grain-fed veal is from animals that are fed a milk-based diet for the first 6 weeks of their life, are then moved onto a grain-based supplement and are culled at 16–18 weeks. Some are kept completely indoors, but generally animals are kept in roomy pens with other calves and have access to sunlight and bedding, which they invariably nibble on. Organically raised veal is more likely to have had something of an outdoors existence and certainly some access to grass. Fans of this style of veal argue that its flavour is more complex and interesting than 'white' veal, yet it still retains the characteristic tenderness for which veal is so enjoyed.

A third type of veal is called 'bob' or 'bobby' veal, from calves that are slaughtered at around 3 weeks of age. In Scotland, 'staggering bob' was once used as slang for a just-born calf, still unable to walk yet slaughtered for its meat. However, it is a mistake to think that the younger the calf, the better the veal — in fact, 'bob' veal is too small and young to have developed any texture or character, and the cuts from these animals are insipid and chewy. Not to mention tiny. These animals are also subject to great stress as they are separated from their mothers and transported for slaughter very young, which also adversely affects their quality.

Nutritional content

Of all the red meats, veal has the least fat. A 115 g (4 oz) serving has, on average, around 5 g (1/8 oz) of fat, yet supplies a massive 32 g (1 1/4 oz) of protein and a weeny 775 kilojoules. Veal is also a good source of vitamins A, B2, B3, B6 and B12, and minerals such as copper, selenium and iron. It is particularly rich in magnesium and zinc.

Buying and storing

When buying veal, remember that the whiter the meat, the higher the proportion of milk in the calf's diet. Exclusively milk-fed veal will be extremely pale. The meat from grain-fed, 'pasture-fed', 'rose' or organic veal has rosy-pink flesh with fat that is creamy white to ivory; any marrow should be dark pink. The cuts won't be as large as those from formula-fed veal. (There's no point looking for marbled veal as the animals are slaughtered too young for any marbling to develop.)

Avoid meat that is very dark or has yellowish fat. The meat should be moist, but not wet, tacky or slimy. As with all meat-buying, cultivate a good butcher who truly knows his wares and can procure the best-quality veal — you may even need to pre-order certain cuts.

Veal is more perishable than other red meats. It doesn't need to be aged as it isn't 'tough' enough to benefit from this, so it is very fresh indeed when you buy it. Take it out of any plastic wrapping, place larger cuts or chops on a tray or large plate, cover with fresh plastic, then refrigerate in the coolest part of the fridge for no longer than 2 days. Pour off any bloody juices that accumulate as these can taint the meat. Minced (ground) veal should be stored in a covered bowl or container and used within a day.

Well wrapped in layers of plastic, to insulate the delicate flesh from the rigours of freezing, veal will freeze for up to 6 months, but is best used within 3 months.

Cuts of veal

Cuts of veal are essentially the same as those from beef, only much smaller.

From the veal forequarters come the neck and shoulder, shank and breast, all excellent cuts for braising; the breast is also good for stuffing and poaching. The shoulder yields shoulder chops for grilling and, if left whole, makes a wonderful roast. Also from here is the rib — the source of luxurious rib chops and roasting meat (the rack), depending on how it is cut.

From the hindquarters come the more expensive cuts such as the loin, which can be cut into chops or left whole to roast; the chops are the equivalent of beef porterhouse or T-bone steaks. If boned-out whole, the butcher can extract the tenderloin and top loin from here; these can in turn be cut into steaks or medallions. Then there's the round (rump), or leg, which can be roasted whole or cut into thin slices to be cooked as escalopes (also called scallopine or schnitzels). In Britain the leg cuts are variously called the silverside, thick flank and topside. When rolled and tied, the topside is sometimes called a 'cushion' of veal.

There is also good eating to be had on the hind shank, the cut best known for its use in osso bucco. Once quite a cheap dish to make, osso bucco has enjoyed wild popularity on restaurant menus over the past decade and the cost of shanks has risen exponentially. For osso bucco, do buy rear shank pieces and preferably those cut from the top of the leg — the lower ones are stringier and much less meaty.

Also perfect for braising, if you can find it, is the flank — it is often minced (ground). This is not a particularly thick cut, but can be rolled and poached, or cubed for stews.

Minced veal has excellent binding qualities as it is rich in collagen, making it an excellent base for meatballs, stuffings and meatloaves.

Calves' feet are among the best sources of gelatine and are often added, split in two, to a braise or stew to add body to the cooking liquid. Before the days of powdered gelatine, calves' feet were used in aspics and jellies, both sweet and savoury; one calf's foot is sufficient to firmly set a little over 500 ml (17 fl oz/2 cups) of liquid (it has to be simmered in the liquid until the collagen has broken down into gelatine).

COOKING VEAL

Many of the world's celebrated veal dishes come from the Italians, Germans, Austrians and French: the Milanese osso bucco (literally 'hollow bone' — veal shanks braised in a tomato-based sauce and spiked with lemony gremolata); the Austrian wiener schnitzel (crumbed and fried slices of the tenderest veal, often served with just a wedge of lemon for squeezing over), *blanquette de veau* (a white, creamy stew of veal, mushrooms and onions; see page 133) or *paupiettes* of veal (thin slices of veal rolled around a savoury filling, then pan-fried). Then there's *vitello tonnato* (poached veal served cold and slathered with tuna mayonnaise; see page 137), saltimbocca (thin slices of veal cooked with sage and prosciutto; see page 134), and *cima alla Genovese*, or stuffed veal breast, the crowning glory of Ligurian cuisine and a Christmas-table favourite.

Veal partners equally well with piquant sauces and strong flavours and the richness of cream and butter. Inherently tender and lean, many veal cuts are perfect for grilled and fried dishes. However, veal is also suitable for stews and braising — it contains large amounts of collagen which, with long, slow cooking, breaks down and makes the meat gorgeously sticky and lush, and the cooking liquid rich and full-bodied. Large, tender pieces of veal, either on or off the bone, make memorable roasts, while some of the cheaper and more under-rated cuts, such as breast, are delicious poached.

Roasting veal

The best cuts for roasting are the whole loin, shoulder, round (or rump) and, if you can find one, the entire rear leg, also called a steamship roast. The whole rib section, which makes a spectacular standing roast and is often called a rack of veal, has eight ribs and is one of the best choices for roasting.

Veal is suitable for slow or fast-roasting, although take care when fast-roasting that the meat doesn't dry out. To avoid this, the initial searing temperature should be a little lower than that for beef — around 190°C (375°F/Gas 5). Because it is a lean meat, the surface may need protecting with an added layer of fat — very thin slices of pork back fat (from your butcher) or slices of good bacon or pancetta — to stop it drying out.

Medium–rare, and well rested, is as rare as you should cook your veal; arguably it tastes better when cooked to medium. (Its texture and flavour are not robust enough to serve it rare.) Aim for an internal temperature of 55–60°C (130–140°F) and certainly no higher than 70°C (150°F).

Braising veal

With the exception of the rib and loin cuts, veal lends itself beautifully to braising and stewing. The best cuts include the shoulder, neck, shanks (the rear shanks are meatier, while the fore shanks are a little more tender), the breast, flank and silverside (which is cut from the top of the leg). Buy whole pieces for braising and cut them to size yourself — this way you can be sure of what you are buying, which you can't with pre-cut 'veal stewing' mixtures.

Larger cuts of veal (left whole) are also perfect for pot-roasting, especially the breast, round (rump) and most particularly the shoulder, which are all wonderfully rich in collagen and make for a lovely, full-bodied sauce. To cook a bone-in shoulder whole by other methods presents carving difficulties, but if you pot-roast it the meat will be practically falling off the bones by the time it is cooked. Otherwise, get a boneless shoulder or breast and have it tied into a neat, tight shape so it will hold its shape while it cooks whole. A breast is best purchased whole (or, more accurately, as a 'half breast') and boned by your butcher. It has an irregular shape and is suited to stuffing before being rolled, tied and then pot-roasted or poached. Have your butcher cut a pocket for stuffing into the breast when you buy it.

Brown the entire piece of meat to be pot-roasted in a little oil or butter in a saucepan just large enough to hold it snugly. Add some vegetables and aromatics (garlic, bacon, pancetta, mushrooms, thyme, celery, carrot) and 250–500 ml (9–17 fl oz/1–2 cups) of liquid (stock, wine, tomatoes) — the meat should barely be half covered. Cover with a tight-fitting lid and slowly simmer on the stove or in a 150°C (300°F/Gas 2) oven, turning the meat regularly. When the veal is cooked, skim the fat from the liquid and boil the juices to reduce them. You can enrich these with a splash of cream if you like.

Frying and grilling veal

There are fewer cuts of meat more perfect for shallow-frying than the veal escalope (also called scallopine or schnitzel). These are rarely more than 1 cm (5/8 inch) thick, enabling them to cook quickly enough that they won't toughen or dry out before they are cooked in the centre. (Don't choose very thin pieces as these will dry out and harden while cooking.) All veal is expensive, but with escalopes there is no waste (no fat or sinews), and 115 g (4 oz) is a generous serving per person.

Veal is a moist meat and needs to be patted dry before cooking — take special care not to neglect this step when frying escalopes or they'll stick to the pan (if you are coating them, the coating will also become wet and gluggy). It seems to be common practice to pound such slim veal cuts with a mallet to tenderise them, but if you buy them from a reputable butcher who cuts them from just one muscle, pounding isn't necessary and can destroy their delicate texture by turning the muscle fibres to mush. Buy escalopes from a reputable butcher who will cut to order from a whole cut (or buy a piece of veal and cut them yourself). Avoid escalopes cut across several muscles — you can recognise these by their lines of connective tissue. Often, meat retailers will mallet such pieces to disguise the joins of muscles. These will buckle and toughen as they cook because the various muscles have differing points of tenderness and won't cook evenly. A good butcher will cut escalopes from properly separated leg muscles, at a slight angle across the grain. The very best come from the top loin, tenderloin or any of the separated leg muscles. You can get escalopes cut from the shoulder, but these will be tougher and are better braised.

Escalopes can be lightly dusted in flour before cooking (to help protect the meat). Butter is a good cooking medium for veal as its richness complements the flavour, but you can mix in olive oil if you worry about the butter burning. Briefly cook over medium heat to minimise moisture loss and the risk of drying out — 2 minutes on each side is usually sufficient. Once cooked, remove the meat to a warm place, pour the excess fat from the pan, then deglaze the pan with a little stock or wine. Once this has reduced, a delicious, creamy sauce can be made by adding some cream and flavouring this with mustard, lemon, green peppercorns, capers, a herb such as thyme, basil or tarragon, or a splash of balsamic vinegar.

Medallions of veal, cut from the tenderloin, boneless loin or boneless rib, are also perfect for frying, as are chops and cutlets (cut either from the bone-in loin, rib or shoulder). Veal is delicate and does not need to be as deeply browned as beef, so don't fry these cuts over too fierce a heat. Also, if they are more than 4 cm (1½ inches) thick they will take too long to cook and may become hard and tough. Cook medallions until juicy-pink in the middle (medium–rare to medium, or to 55–60°C/130–140°F) rather than rare — they just won't taste great if undercooked.

Overhead grilling (broiling) is not recommended for very lean meats such as veal as it tends to dry them out. However, chargrilling on a ridged grill pan or on a medium–hot barbecue are excellent methods for cooking tender veal cutlets, chops and medallions. As with frying, just don't grill them over a very fiery heat, don't have your cutlets cut too thick, and don't overcook (or undercook) the meat.

Poaching

A number of veal cuts are well suited to poaching, including the under-rated breast, the shoulder and the hind-leg shin (sometimes called the knuckle). As with other meats, poaching works best for intact, large cuts.

Choose a saucepan that is just big enough to snugly accommodate the piece of meat — if the pan is too large, you will need to add too much liquid and by doing so dilute the final flavour. Immerse the veal in the liquid just after it has come to a gentle simmer (rather than putting it into cold liquid and bringing it to a simmer) — this helps 'seal' the meat. Veal will give up quite a lot of scum, which should be ladled off. Its delicate flavour means subtle poaching liquids are best — chicken or veal stock, or even water with a little white wine. To this you can add some simple aromatics such as bay leaves, thyme sprigs, clove-studded onions, and vegetables such as carrot. These will create a fairly neutral flavour profile for building a delicious sauce when the meat has finished poaching. Remove the cooked meat from the saucepan, skim the cooking liquid of fat and any surface impurities, then strain through a fine sieve and boil over medium–high heat to reduce the volume. The sauce can then be thickened with a simple paste of flour and butter, enriched with cream, or flavoured with sautéed mushrooms, lemon, tarragon, parsley, capers or the like. Slices of the poached meat can be gently reheated in the sauce, if necessary.

Uccelletti scappati

Serves 4

650 g (1 lb 7 oz) veal escalopes
90 g (3 1/4 oz) pancetta, thinly sliced, plus a 90 g (3 1/4 oz) piece of pancetta, cut into 24 cubes
50 sage leaves, cut in half
75 g (2 1/2 oz) clarified butter
grilled or creamy polenta, to serve (optional)

Soak 12 wooden skewers in cold water for 1 hour to prevent scorching.

Working in batches, place the veal slices between two sheets of plastic wrap and pound to an even thickness using a meat pounder. Cut the veal into 6 x 3 cm (2 1/2 x 1 1/4 inch) rectangles, then trim the pancetta slices to the same size.

Lay the veal slices on a board and season with freshly ground black pepper. Roll each veal slice up, starting from one of the shortest ends.

Thread a cube of pancetta onto a skewer, followed by a sage leaf. Thread the skewer through a veal roll to stop it unrolling. Thread four more veal rolls onto the skewer, then a sage leaf and another cube of pancetta. Continue threading the skewers until all the ingredients are used.

Heat the butter in a large frying pan. When it starts to foam, add the skewers in batches and cook over high heat for 12 minutes, or until cooked through, turning several times. Season lightly with sea salt and freshly ground black pepper. Serve with grilled or creamy polenta, if desired.

Veal goulash

Serves 4

50 g (1¾ oz) butter
750 g (1 lb 10 oz) boneless veal shoulder, cut into 3 cm (1¼ inch) chunks
2 red onions, chopped
2 garlic cloves, chopped
1 tablespoon Hungarian paprika
½ teaspoon caraway seeds
4 tomatoes
1 marjoram sprig
125 g (4½ oz) button mushrooms, trimmed and wiped clean, large ones cut in half
1 green capsicum (pepper), chopped
1 red capsicum (pepper), chopped
1 tablespoon tomato paste (concentrated purée)
pasta or boiled potatoes, to serve
sour cream, to serve

Preheat the oven to 160°C (315°F/Gas 2–3). Heat the butter in a 2.5 litre (87 fl oz/10 cup) flameproof casserole dish. Add the veal in batches and cook over medium heat for 5 minutes, turning to brown all over. Remove and set aside.

Add the onion and garlic to the casserole dish and sauté for 5 minutes. Add the paprika and caraway seeds, stir to coat the onion, then sauté for a further 5 minutes.

Meanwhile, using a small, sharp knife, score a small cross in the base of each tomato. Plunge into boiling water for 20 seconds, then drain and plunge into iced water to cool. Peel the skin away from the cross, then roughly chop the flesh and add to the casserole.

Return the veal to the casserole. Stir in the marjoram, mushrooms, capsicum, tomato paste and 125 ml (4 fl oz/½ cup) water. Cover and bake for 1¾ hours, or until the veal is tender.

Discard the marjoram sprig, then season the goulash well with sea salt and freshly ground black pepper. Serve with pasta or boiled potatoes, with a dollop of sour cream.

Blanquette de veau

Serves 6

800 g (1 lb 12 oz) boneless veal shoulder, cut into 3 cm (1¼ inch) cubes
1 litre (35 fl oz/4 cups) veal or beef stock
4 cloves
½ large onion
1 small carrot, roughly chopped
1 leek, white part only, rinsed well and roughly chopped
1 celery stalk, roughly chopped
1 bay leaf
30 g (1 oz) butter
3 tablespoons plain (all-purpose) flour
1 tablespoon lemon juice
1 egg yolk, mixed with 2½ tablespoons thick (double/heavy) cream
steamed white rice or boiled new potatoes, to serve

ONION GARNISH
250 g (9 oz) baby onions
10 g (¼ oz) butter
1 teaspoon caster (superfine) sugar

MUSHROOM GARNISH
10 g (¼ oz) butter
2 teaspoons lemon juice
150 g (5½ oz) button mushrooms, trimmed

Put the veal in a large saucepan, cover with cold water and bring to the boil. Drain, rinse well and drain again. Return to the pan and add the stock. Press the cloves into the onion and add to the pan with the remaining vegetables and bay leaf.

Bring to the boil, then reduce the heat. Cover and simmer for 40–60 minutes, or until the veal is tender, skimming the surface occasionally.

While the veal is simmering, make the onion garnish. Put the onions in a small pan with enough water to half cover them. Add the butter and sugar. Place a round of baking paper directly over the onions. Bring the mixture to a simmer and cook over low heat for 20 minutes, or until the water has evaporated and the onions are tender.

To make the mushroom garnish, half-fill a small saucepan with water and bring to the boil. Add the butter, lemon juice and mushrooms and simmer for 3 minutes, or until the mushrooms are tender. Drain the mushrooms, discarding the liquid.

When the veal is tender, remove it from the saucepan and keep warm while making the sauce. Strain the cooking liquid into a bowl and discard the vegetables.

Melt the butter in a large saucepan. Add the flour and stir until a smooth paste forms, then stir over low heat for 3 minutes — do not allow the paste to brown. Remove from the heat and gradually add the veal cooking liquid, stirring well after each addition until smooth.

Place the pan back over the heat. Whisking constantly, bring the sauce to the boil, then reduce the heat to low. Stirring occasionally, simmer for 8 minutes, or until the sauce is thick enough to coat the back of the spoon. Add the lemon juice and season well with sea salt and freshly ground black pepper. Quickly stir in the egg yolk and cream, then add the veal and the onion and mushroom garnishes. Reheat gently, without boiling.

Serve with steamed white rice or boiled new potatoes.

Saltimbocca

Serves 4

- 8 small veal escalopes
- 8 slices of prosciutto
- 8 sage leaves
- 2 tablespoons olive oil
- 60 g (2¼ oz) butter
- 185 ml (6 fl oz/¾ cup) dry marsala or dry white wine

Place the veal slices between two sheets of plastic wrap and pound using a meat pounder until about 5 mm (¼ inch) thick. Season lightly with sea salt and freshly ground black pepper.

Cut the prosciutto slices to the same size as the veal. Cover each piece of veal with a prosciutto slice and place a sage leaf in the centre. Secure the sage leaf with a cocktail stick or toothpick.

Heat the olive oil and half the butter in a large frying pan. Add the veal in batches, prosciutto side up, and fry over medium heat for 3–4 minutes, or until the veal is just cooked through. Turn and fry the prosciutto side, transferring each batch to a warm plate.

Pour off the oil from the pan and add the marsala. Bring to the boil and cook over high heat until reduced by half, stirring to loosen any bits stuck to the bottom of the pan. Add the remaining butter and, when it has melted, season the sauce to taste with sea salt and freshly ground black pepper.

Divide the saltimbocca among four warmed plates, remove the cocktail sticks and spoon the sauce over to serve.

Vitello tonnato

Serves 4–6

1.25 kg (2 lb 12 oz) boneless rolled veal roast
500 ml (17 fl oz/2 cups) dry white wine
500 ml (17 fl oz/2 cups) chicken stock
2 garlic cloves, bruised
1 onion, quartered
1 carrot, roughly chopped
1 celery stalk, roughly chopped
2 bay leaves
3 cloves
10 peppercorns
parsley leaves, to garnish
capers, to garnish
thin lemon wedges, to serve

TUNA MAYONNAISE
95 g (3¼ oz) tin of tuna in olive oil
6 anchovy fillets, or to taste
2 egg yolks
2 tablespoons lemon juice
125 ml (4 fl oz/½ cup) olive oil

Put the veal, wine, stock, garlic, onion, carrot, celery, bay leaves, cloves and peppercorns in a stockpot or very large saucepan. Add enough water to come two-thirds up the side of the veal and bring to the boil. Reduce the heat, then cover and simmer for 1¼ hours, or until the veal is tender.

Leave the veal to cool in the liquid for 30 minutes, then remove from the pot. Strain the stock into a clean saucepan, bring to the boil, then cook over medium–high heat until reduced to about 250 ml (9 fl oz/1 cup).

To make the tuna mayonnaise, place the undrained tuna, anchovy fillets, egg yolks and 1 tablespoon of the lemon juice in a blender or food processor and blend until smooth. With the motor running, add the olive oil in a thin, steady stream; do not add the oil too quickly or the sauce will split. Gradually add enough of the reduced stock to thin the sauce to a creamy, pouring consistency. Add the remaining lemon juice and season well with sea salt and freshly ground black pepper.

Thinly slice the cooled veal and arrange in overlapping slices on serving plates. Spoon the sauce over, garnish with parsley and capers and serve with lemon wedges.

LEMON AND SAGE MARINATED VEAL CHOPS WITH ROCKET

SERVES 4

4 veal chops, trimmed
2 tablespoons olive oil
1 tablespoon lemon juice
4 lemon zest strips
3 tablespoons roughly chopped sage leaves
3 garlic cloves, bruised
lemon wedges, to serve
crusty bread, to serve

ROCKET SALAD
150 g (5½ oz/1 bunch) rocket (arugula), stalks removed
1 avocado, sliced
1½ tablespoons extra virgin olive oil
2 teaspoons balsamic vinegar

Put the veal in a shallow, non-metallic dish with the olive oil, lemon juice, lemon zest, sage and garlic, turning to coat. Season with freshly ground black pepper, then cover and refrigerate for 4 hours, or overnight.

Preheat a chargrill pan or barbecue chargrill plate to medium–high. Remove the veal from the marinade, season with sea salt and freshly ground black pepper and chargrill for 5–6 minutes on each side, or until cooked to your liking. Transfer to a warm plate, cover loosely with foil and leave to rest in a warm place for 5 minutes.

Meanwhile, make the rocket salad. Put the rocket in a large serving bowl and arrange the avocado over the top. Drizzle with the olive oil and vinegar, season to taste with sea salt and freshly ground black pepper and toss gently.

Divide the veal among four warmed plates, drizzle with any resting juices and serve with the rocket salad, lemon wedges and crusty bread.

Veal schnitzels with warm dill potato salad

Serves 4

DILL POTATO SALAD

2 tablespoons lemon juice
1 1/2 tablespoons finely chopped dill
3 tablespoons virgin olive oil
750 g (1 lb 10 oz) desiree potatoes, scrubbed but not peeled

4 veal leg steaks, about 500 g (1 lb 2 oz) in total
60 g (2 1/4 oz/1/2 cup) plain (all-purpose) flour
2 eggs
100 g (3 1/2 oz/1 cup) dry breadcrumbs
3 tablespoons virgin olive oil
200 g (7 oz) mixed salad leaves

To make the dill potato salad, whisk the lemon juice, dill and olive oil together in a small bowl and set aside. Cook the potatoes in a saucepan of boiling, salted water for 15–20 minutes, or until tender.

Meanwhile, using a meat pounder, beat the veal steaks between two sheets of plastic wrap until 5 mm (1/4 inch) thick. Put the flour in a shallow bowl and season with sea salt and freshly ground black pepper. Crack the eggs into another bowl and lightly beat. Put the breadcrumbs in a separate bowl.

Dust the veal in the flour, shaking off the excess. Dip the veal in the beaten egg, then coat in the breadcrumbs. Place the schnitzels on a baking tray, cover with plastic wrap and freeze for 5 minutes.

Heat the olive oil in a large frying pan. Cook the schnitzels in two batches over medium–high heat for 2–3 minutes on each side, or until golden and cooked through. Drain on paper towels and keep warm.

When the potatoes are tender, drain well, then cut into quarters lengthways. Pour the dill dressing over the potatoes, season with sea salt and freshly ground black pepper and toss gently to combine.

Serve the warm schnitzels on a bed of salad leaves with the potato salad.

Paprika veal with caraway noodles

Serves 4–6

3 tablespoons olive oil
1 kg (2 lb 4 oz) boneless veal shoulder, cut into 2 cm (3/4 inch) cubes
1 large onion, thinly sliced
3 garlic cloves, finely chopped
3 tablespoons Hungarian paprika
1/2 teaspoon caraway seeds
2 x 400 g (14 oz) tins chopped tomatoes, one tin drained
350 g (12 oz) fresh fettuccine
40 g (1 1/2 oz) butter, softened
crusty bread, to serve

Heat half the olive oil in a large saucepan over medium–high heat. Add the veal in batches and cook for 3 minutes, turning to brown all over. Remove from the pan and set aside, also reserving any pan juices.

Heat the remaining olive oil in the pan, add the onion and garlic and cook over medium heat for 5 minutes, or until the onion has softened. Add the paprika and half the caraway seeds and stir for 30 seconds. Add the tomatoes and their liquid, along with 125 ml (4 fl oz/1/2 cup) water. Return the veal to the pan with the pan juices, bring to a gentle simmer, then cover and cook for 1 1/4 hours, or until the veal is tender and the sauce has thickened.

About 15 minutes before the veal is ready, cook the pasta in a saucepan of boiling salted water until *al dente*. Drain, then return to the pan. Stir in the butter and remaining caraway seeds and serve with the veal and crusty bread.

Osso bucco with gremolata

Serves 4

2 tablespoons olive oil
1 onion, finely chopped
1 garlic clove, crushed
1 kg (2 lb 4 oz) osso bucco
2 tablespoons plain (all-purpose) flour
400 g (14 oz) tin chopped tomatoes
250 ml (9 fl oz/1 cup) white wine
250 ml (9 fl oz/1 cup) chicken stock
risotto or steamed white rice, to serve

GREMOLATA
2 tablespoons finely chopped parsley
2 teaspoons grated lemon zest
1 teaspoon finely chopped garlic

Heat half the olive oil in a large shallow flameproof casserole dish. Add the onion and sauté over low heat for 10 minutes, or until soft and golden. Add the garlic and cook for 1 minute, then remove from the dish.

Heat the remaining oil in the casserole dish. Add the veal in batches and brown over medium–high heat for 6–7 minutes, turning once. Remove the veal.

Return the onion to the casserole dish and stir in the flour. Cook for 30 seconds, remove from the heat, then slowly stir in the tomatoes, wine and stock until well combined. Add the veal, place back over the heat and bring to the boil, stirring. Cover, reduce the heat to low and gently simmer for 2½ hours, or until the meat is very tender and almost falling off the bone.

In a small bowl, mix together the gremolata ingredients. Serve the osso bucco on a bed of risotto or steamed white rice, sprinkled with the gremolata.

Cevapcici

Serves 6

500 g (1 lb 2 oz) minced (ground) veal
250 g (9 oz) minced (ground) pork
½ onion, grated
1 garlic clove, crushed
2 tablespoons finely chopped dill
1 tablespoon finely chopped parsley
1½ teaspoons ground coriander
½ teaspoon ground cumin
1 teaspoon paprika
1 teaspoon salt
½ teaspoon freshly ground black pepper
1 teaspoon baking powder
3 tablespoons beef stock
25 g (1 oz/⅓ cup) fresh white breadcrumbs
1 egg, lightly beaten
relish or chutney, to serve

Put all the ingredients, except the relish or chutney, in a large bowl and thoroughly mix together with your hands.

Using wet hands, divide the mixture into 18 equal portions. Roll each portion into a sausage shape about 12 cm (4½ inches) long, placing them on a tray. Cover with plastic wrap and refrigerate for 1 hour.

Heat the grill (broiler) to medium–high. Transfer the sausages to the grill tray and cook for 6–8 minutes, or until cooked through, turning to brown all over.

Serve hot, with your favourite relish or chutney.

Balsamic-roasted veal cutlets with red onion

Serves 4

- $1\frac{1}{2}$ tablespoons olive oil
- 8 veal cutlets
- 4 unpeeled garlic cloves
- 1 red onion, cut into thin wedges
- 1 tablespoon chopped rosemary
- 250 g (9 oz) cherry tomatoes
- 3 tablespoons balsamic vinegar
- 2 teaspoons soft brown sugar
- 2 tablespoons chopped flat-leaf (Italian) parsley

Preheat the oven to 200°C (400°F/Gas 6). Heat the olive oil in a large frying pan over medium heat. Add the veal in batches and cook for 4 minutes on each side, or until browned.

Arrange the cutlets in a single layer in a large, shallow roasting tin. Add the garlic cloves, onion, rosemary, cherry tomatoes, vinegar and sugar. Season well with sea salt and freshly ground black pepper, then cover tightly with foil and roast for 15 minutes.

Remove the foil and roast for a further 10–15 minutes, or until cooked through — the actual cooking time will vary depending on the thickness of the cutlets. Remove from the oven, cover loosely with foil and leave to rest in a warm place for 4–5 minutes.

Transfer the cutlets, garlic, onion and tomatoes to four warmed plates. Stir the pan juices until well combined. Spoon over the cutlets, then sprinkle with the parsley.

PARMESAN AND ROSEMARY-CRUSTED VEAL CHOPS WITH SALSA ROSSA

SERVES 4

SALSA ROSSA
3 tablespoons olive oil
3 large onions, finely sliced
3 large red capsicums (peppers), cut into 1 cm (1/2 inch) wide strips
1/4 teaspoon chilli flakes
400 g (14 oz) tin chopped tomatoes

4 veal chops, trimmed
150 g (5 1/2 oz/2 cups) fresh white breadcrumbs
75 g (2 1/2 oz/3/4 cup) grated parmesan cheese
1 tablespoon finely chopped rosemary
2 eggs
3 tablespoons olive oil
60 g (2 1/4 oz) butter
4 garlic cloves, bruised

To make the salsa rossa, heat the olive oil in a heavy-based frying pan. Add the onion and cook over medium heat for 5 minutes, or until soft but not browned. Add the capsicum and cook, stirring occasionally, for 30 minutes, or until very soft. Add the chilli flakes and tomatoes and season with sea salt. Simmer for a further 25 minutes, or until the sauce has thickened and the oil has separated from the tomatoes. Check the seasoning and adjust if necessary. Keep warm.

Meanwhile, using a meat pounder, flatten the veal until 1 cm (1/2 inch) thick. Pat dry with paper towels.

Combine the breadcrumbs, parmesan and rosemary in a shallow bowl. Beat the eggs in a separate bowl and lightly season with sea salt and freshly ground black pepper.

Dip each veal chop in the beaten egg, draining off the excess, then press both sides firmly in the breadcrumb mixture.

Heat the olive oil and butter in a large, heavy-based frying pan over low heat. Add the garlic and cook until golden. Discard the garlic.

Increase the heat to medium, add the veal and cook for 4–5 minutes on each side, or until the crumbs are golden and crisp and the meat is just cooked through. Remove to a warmed plate, cover loosely with foil and leave to rest for 4–5 minutes.

Transfer the veal to four warmed plates, season lightly and serve with the salsa rossa.

Roast veal stuffed with ham and spinach

Serves 4

800 g (1 lb 12 oz/2 bunches) English spinach
2 garlic cloves, crushed
2 tablespoons finely chopped parsley
2 teaspoons dijon mustard
100 g (3½ oz) ham, chopped
finely grated zest of 1 lemon
600 g (1 lb 5 oz) piece of boneless veal loin or fillet, butterflied to measure 30 x 15 cm (12 x 6 inches) — ask your butcher to do this
6 slices of bacon
2 tablespoons olive oil
50 g (1¾ oz) butter
8 small unpeeled potatoes
200 ml (7 fl oz) dry madeira
8 shallots
16 baby carrots, trimmed

Preheat the oven to 170°C (325°F/Gas 3). Thoroughly wash the spinach and place in a large saucepan with just the water clinging to the leaves. Cover and steam for 2 minutes, or until just wilted. Drain, cool and squeeze dry with your hands. Chop the spinach and toss in a bowl with the garlic, parsley, mustard, ham and lemon zest. Season well with sea salt and freshly ground black pepper.

Spread the spinach mixture over the centre of the veal. Starting from one of the shorter sides, roll the veal up like a Swiss roll (jelly roll). Wrap the bacon around the veal, overlapping the slices slightly. Season well. Using kitchen string, tie the veal at 5 cm (2 inch) intervals to secure the bacon and form a neat shape.

Heat the olive oil and half the butter in a large frying pan. Add the potatoes and sauté over medium heat for 8–10 minutes, or until browned, then transfer to a roasting tin.

Add the veal to the frying pan and cook over medium–high heat for 8 minutes, turning to brown all over. Remove and place on top of the potatoes. Add 4 tablespoons of the madeira to the frying pan and boil, stirring to loosen any bits stuck to the bottom of the pan, then pour over the veal.

Roast the veal for 30 minutes, then cover with foil and roast for a further 45 minutes, or until the juices run clear when tested with a skewer in the thickest part. Add the shallots to the roasting tin 30 minutes before the end of cooking time, and the carrots 15 minutes before the end.

Remove the veal to a warm plate, cover loosely with foil and leave to rest in a warm place for 10–15 minutes. Roast the vegetables a little longer if they are not tender, then remove from the roasting tin and keep warm.

Place the roasting tin over medium heat and add the remaining madeira. Bring to the boil, then add the remaining butter and season to taste.

Slice the veal thickly and arrange on four warmed plates with the vegetables. Drizzle with some of the madeira sauce and serve the remainder separately.

offal

The word 'offal' derives literally from the parts of an animal that 'fall off' the butcher's block (feet, heads, wing tips etc). In fifteenth-century England, the literal meaning shifted and offal came to define the various innards of animals, which is how we understand the term today.

In Rome, offal is fondly called *il quinto quarto* or 'the fifth quarter', a nice way to describe all those parts that don't belong to the four quarters of a carcass. More often though, offal is euphemistically referred to as 'variety' meat.

Many modern cooks are ambivalent about offal. There are those who adore it and those who find the very thought of it stomach-churning. Until quite recently, absolutely all parts of an animal were used, and organ meat was regarded as a legitimate meat in its own right. The concept of dining upon selective parts of an animal carcass is a fairly modern one — a result of increasing affluence and the ever-cheapening of prime red meat.

Throughout continental Europe, the British Isles, all through Asia, the Middle East and also South America, offal dishes abound. Think of the Scots' beloved haggis (sheep's stomach stuffed with oatmeal and other sheep bits such as lungs and spleen, then boiled), the various blood sausages of the world, and pâtés (typically made with liver). The French delight in *andouillette*, a sausage in which pig or calf intestines provide both the casing and the filling. They also love the feet, ears and tail of pigs. Tripe lyonnaise (a buttery sauté of onion and fine strips of cooked tripe finished with vinegar), creamy fricassees of sweetbreads, and pan-fried kidneys and liver are also popular. 'Head cheese' or brawn, a deeply savoury jelly containing the chopped meat of a boiled pig's head, is still enjoyed in France and Britain. The Spaniards cook bull's testicles and cow's udders; in Sicily you can buy a spleen sandwich (*pane cu i milza*) on the street, while in Rome, *pajata* (intestines from calves so young they are still full of their mother's milk when cooked) are a speciality.

In Greece, Turkey and parts of the Middle East, whole lamb's heads are a delicacy. Peruvians skewer bits of goat or cow heart, marinate them in spices and vinegar and barbecue them — a popular street food called *antichuchos*. Americans might be surprised to know that the famed Philadelphian concoction 'scrapple' is based on scraps of cooked pork, commonly including the brain, heart and liver.

Ironically, certain offal dishes have become sought-after menu items in fancy restaurants in the developed world. Top chefs pay premiums for quality organ meats such as lamb's brains, sweetbreads, the best veal liver and kidneys. This has made these types of offal quite difficult to procure by those not in the restaurant trade and has driven prices up dramatically.

Nutritional value

Most offal is highly nutritious, but with the exception of heart rather high in cholesterol. Liver and kidney are rich in iron; liver is also an excellent source of selenium, folate and vitamin A, while kidneys are rich in vitamin A, folate and vitamin B12. Heart is high in copper, iron, vitamin B, phosphorous and potassium. Tripe offers good amounts of selenium, zinc, phosphorous, potassium and vitamin B12. Brains are rich in selenium, B12 and B6 and niacin, while sweetbreads — one of the few animal products containing vitamin C — also has good amounts of niacin, zinc and phosphorous. Offal meats contain quite high levels of purines, which gout sufferers are advised to avoid.

Buying and storing offal

'Fresh fresh fresh' should be the offal-buyer's mantra; offal deteriorates very quickly and is not the stuff to purchase from places that offer meat of uncertain provenance. Think of what offal is: it's glands and organs, many of which filter toxins, infectious organisms and waste. When a carcass is rejected by abattoir inspectors it is often the beast's organs that indicate illness or contamination. Scrupulously source your offal from a specialist butcher, who in turn sources it from organic or free-range farmers.

Fresh offal shouldn't smell unpleasant and should appear firm and glossy. If it looks dry, overly dark (in the case of kidneys and liver) or is starting to shrivel or smells strongly, don't have a bar of it. Butchers who sell to Greek, Arab, Chinese, Vietnamese or South American communities are often great sources of offal; you're likely to find a good variety of very fresh organ meats, thanks to decent turnover.

Buy offal on the day you wish to cook it, or store it in the refrigerator for no longer than a day — two at a pinch, and only if you are completely sure it is fresh. Offal can be frozen for up to three months; most types are quite delicate so wrap them very well in layers of plastic to avoid freezer burn.

TYPES OF OFFAL

From cocks' combs to ox tails, the range of offal is vast indeed. The following are the most readily available and most widely cooked.

Liver

Livers most easily sourced are chicken, duck, calf (veal), lamb and pig. Ox and pig livers are too strong for most palates and require soaking in milk and long braising — but they can be exquisitely tender and tasty if they are absolutely fresh, and from an animal that was properly raised (not pumped full of additive-laden feed). Pig's livers are often used in pâtés and terrines.

Liver from younger animals has a mild flavour and soft texture, which is why veal and lamb's liver are so popular. If possible buy a whole liver, so you can make neat, even slices for perfect cooking. First peel off the fine outer membrane, being careful not to puncture or otherwise damage the very delicate flesh. (If the membrane is left on, the meat will curl up as it cooks.) Trim off any tubes and bits of thick, hard tissue. Use a large, very sharp knife to neatly slice the liver about 1 cm (1/2 inch) thick. Pan-fry or grill for no more than 4 minutes (less if it is thinner), so it is still pink and juicy in the middle. Never cook liver all the way through (unless braising pig or ox liver) as it will be very unappetising — the main reason for the widespread liver revulsion that exists today!

Liver is delicious with the assertive flavours of browned onions, balsamic or red wine vinegar, sage, mustard, garlic, brandy, mushrooms and rosemary.

Chicken giblets

The giblets of a chicken are the kidney, liver, heart and gizzards (in France they include the feet, head and wings too). Often, when you buy a chicken for roasting or boiling, these parts have been left in the body cavity; canny cooks know to use these bits in a stuffing. You can also buy poultry offal from Asian butchers, as Asian cooks have devised some excellent ways with these meats; generally they sell the hearts and gizzards as giblets.

The livers are particularly delicious and their sweet mildness will sway even the most determined non-offal eater. They are most famously used in pâtés and in the celebrated Jewish dish of chopped liver, but are also fabulous when sautéed and included in pasta sauces, or served atop a toss of green leaves as a warm salad. Or they can be treated just like veal or lamb liver — tossed in a pan with onions, mushrooms or spinach, flavoured with a hit of rosemary, thyme or oregano, and finished with a splash of good vinegar and/or cream and served on toast as a light dinner or an entrée.

Pan-frying is the best way to cook chicken (and duck) livers, but they can also be grilled. First trim them of any membranes and greenish bits (the latter are bile stains and incredibly bitter). It's easiest to cut the two big lobes of liver where they meet in the middle as they are connected by tough, stringy tissue. If the gall bladder is still attached, carefully remove it.

Blot the livers dry with a paper towel and, if you like, lightly dredge in flour. Pan-fry for 3–4 minutes over reasonably high heat, turning often so they cook evenly. Whatever you do, don't cook them past medium — they must be a little pink in the middle at least, or they will be dry and uninteresting. The more cooked they are, the firmer they'll feel — with practice, you can tell if they are ready by giving them a push with your finger.

Brains

Brains really separate the offal men from the offal boys: there is perhaps no more contentious food. Those most commonly enjoyed are lamb and calf brains, with their mild, sweetish flavour and rich, creamy texture. Fresh brains are rather hard to come by, being in hot demand by professional chefs. However, they are often frozen in packets of six. You are most likely to find lamb's brains at your butcher.

To prepare brains, make sure they are thoroughly thawed, if frozen, and soak in several changes of cold water for 30 minutes, or until the water is clear. Carefully peel away the fine outer membrane, along with any chips of bone and bloody bits, then soak for an additional hour in lightly salted cold water in the refrigerator. Cook them in a deep pan of barely simmering chicken or veal stock (or court bouillon) for 5 minutes, or until just firm. Do not boil them or you will destroy their special texture. Carefully remove with a slotted spoon, drain well, then cool. The brains can then be sautéed, coated in seasoned flour and fried, lightly crumbed and deep-fried, or reheated in a delicate cream sauce. They can also be poached in wine or a sauce, or chopped and formed into fritters and croquettes. Brains take well to the full, distinctive flavours of capers, lemon, burnt butter, mild vinegars and mustards, red wine, spinach, watercress and mushrooms.

Sweetbreads

No-one quite knows where the name 'sweetbreads' came from or how it came to be applied to two glands that come from the heart and throat area of lambs and calves. These glands disappear as the animal ages. Sweetbreads are largish and pale and can appear a bit raggedy around the edges. They are always sold together and are prepared identically. Sweetbreads require advance preparation, which could explain why they aren't more popular with home cooks, although the preparation is more tedious than difficult. They are, however, highly sought after by the restaurant trade.

Sweetbreads should be soaked for 2–3 hours in several changes of cold water, until the water is clear. Place them in a saucepan, cover with fresh cold water or cold chicken or veal stock and bring to a gentle simmer. Cook calf sweetbreads for 5 minutes and lamb ones for 2–3 minutes, then drain well and leave until cool enough to handle. Using your hands, remove any fat, sinewy bits or tubes, but try to leave most of the outer membrane intact to hold the cooked sweetbread together. Some recipes call for the sweetbreads to then be wrapped in a cloth, lightly weighed down and left for 3–4 hours to form a compact, neat shape.

Sweetbreads are generally cooked in creamy, fricassee-style sauces, dusted in seasoned flour and pan-fried until crisp on the outside, or lightly crumbed and deep-fried and served with a sauce. Compatible flavours and ingredients are those that help complement their richness — capers, gherkins, parsley, mushrooms, mild mustard, lemon, orange, sorrel, green peppercorns.

Tongue

The sight of a big, ungainly, uncooked ox tongue can be a confronting one. But cook it to silky tenderness and you've got one of the world's strongest cases for mind-over-matter — tongue is delicious. In parts of Asia even duck tongues are prized! The tongue is a muscle, and those of the ox, calf and lamb are popular. Pig tongues are seldom eaten for their own sake but rather with other meats, most famously in brawn. Tongue is very easy to cook and quite versatile as it can be served hot or cold.

Ox (beef) tongues can be purchased fresh or pickled; the latter have been treated with a salted brine which helps preserve them. You may have to specially order fresh tongue from your butcher — it should be an appealing greyish pink, feel firm and have no strong odours.

Fresh or pickled, ox tongue should be soaked for several hours in cold water before cooking. Pickled tongue should then be simmered in a large saucepan of unsalted water — and fresh tongue in lightly salted water — for 2 1/2 hours, or until tender. Lamb's tongue will be tender after 30–40 minutes.

Drain well (reserve the liquid if you want to jelly the tongue), then remove the thick, raspy, inedible skin on the tongue while the tongue is still hot — once cool, it is almost impossible to remove. (Skin that just won't come off can indicate the tongue is not completely cooked.) Trim off any gristly bits at the root of the tongue and remove any small throat bones. The tongue can then be pressed and jellied and served in slices with salads or on sandwiches, or simply cooled and served cold in salads or with simple boiled vegetables or pickles. They can be chopped and incorporated with a sauce into tagines (see page 166) and stews. Slices or chunks can be gently reheated in piquant sauces. Tender, cooked lamb's tongues can be thinly sliced lengthways, coated with fresh breadcrumbs, then pan-fried — they are delicious with home-made tartare sauce and a wedge of lemon.

Sharpish flavours seem to best complement tongue's smooth, rich, sweet meatiness, such as home-made tomato sauce, Italian-style sweet and sour sauce (containing wine vinegar, raisins, green olives, honey or sugar and anchovies), perky salsa verde, vinegary braised cabbage, mellow onion marmalade and sauces spiced with cumin, paprika, cayenne and ginger.

Tripe

American chef Thomas Keller, in his book *The French Laundry*, wrote that 'preparing tripe is a transcendental act; to take what is normally thrown away and, with skill and knowledge, turn it into something exquisite'. Tripe can indeed be exquisite, but many people can't get past the fact that it is the stomach lining of cows (or sheep and pigs).

There are three main types of beef tripe, from the first three stomachs of a cow. The first stomach, the rumen, is where blanket or smooth tripe is derived. Honeycomb (named for the texture of its raised, patterned surface, and also called pocket tripe since it is shaped like a pocket when whole) comes from the second stomach, the reticulum, and is the most popular. Bible or book tripe comes from the third stomach (the omasum) and is the most delicate. Most tripe sold has been bleached in a mild peroxide solution and blanched, giving it a milky colour. Bleached tripe can be simmered or braised to tenderness in around an hour — don't overcook it or you'll have stringy mush. Onions, vinegar, mint, parsley, thyme, bay leaves, tomatoes, garlic, bacon, cider and parmesan are all flavours that complement tripe.

Kidneys

In James Joyce's novel *Ulysses*, a character declares that 'he liked grilled mutton kidneys which gave to his palate a fine tang of faintly scented urine'. And it is this very tang that puts many off eating kidneys. When they're fresh and correctly prepared, kidneys have a distinctive taste and texture that is utterly delicious. The urine whiff that even fresh kidneys give off varies in intensity. Kidneys from younger animals are most sought after as their flavour is milder and their texture more delicate. Pig's kidneys are the strongest tasting and can be quite bitter; ox kidneys are tough, but very good when cooked slowly in small pieces (as in steak and kidney pudding). Most kidneys are sold removed from their surrounding thick casing of protective fat (called suet and used, grated, as an ingredient in traditional baking).

Buy kidneys whole if you can. Choose ones that are firm and shiny — avoid any that are darkening or crinkling around the edges, or smell strong. To prepare them, carefully remove the fine outer membrane. For grilling or frying, cut lamb kidneys in half lengthways to give two flattish, kidney-bean shaped pieces and cut out the tough, fatty core. Slice calf kidneys widthways into 1–1.5 cm (1/2–5/8 inch) slices and remove the hard core from each piece. Sauté, grill or barbecue lamb or calf kidneys for 1–2 minutes on each side and briefly rest before serving. They should still be a little pink in the middle.

If older kidneys are to be braised, cut them into small pieces and cook them slowly and thoroughly for tenderness.

Kidneys go well with bacon, mustard, rosemary, golden onions, mustard, worcestershire sauce, sage and sweet masala.

Cheeks

Although a muscle meat, cheeks are classified as offal because they come from the head of a beast. Beef cheeks have become popular in fashionable restaurants for their seductively melting qualities. Beef cheeks come from a very hard-working muscle and require long, slow, moist cooking to become tender. It is best to buy them on the day you plan to prepare them. They should be deep red and fresh smelling; remove excess fat before cooking.

Beef cheeks go best with classic, beef-braising flavours such as red wine, mustard, mushrooms, garlic, rosemary, thyme, chestnuts, juniper berries, dried beans, salted meats such as bacon, pancetta or prosciutto, and sweet root vegetables like parsnip and celeriac. Cheeks also take well to the flavours of the Moroccan tagine: cinnamon, ginger, cumin, saffron, chilli and honey, plus rich fruits such as prunes, quinces, dried apricots and raisins.

Oxtails

These can be difficult to get fresh, but frozen ones are also available. Oxtails are sought after for their incomparable braising qualities — with their large ratios of bone and connective tissue to meat (and good quantities of fat), the texture of braised oxtail is incomparable.

Chicken liver and Grand Marnier pâté

Serves 8

750 g (1 lb 10 oz) chicken livers, well trimmed (see page 153)
250 ml (9 fl oz/1 cup) milk
200 g (7 oz) butter, softened
4 spring onions (scallions), finely chopped
2 tablespoons Grand Marnier
2 tablespoons orange juice concentrate
toast or baguette, to serve

JELLY

2 teaspoons orange juice concentrate
2 teaspoons Grand Marnier
150 ml (5 fl oz) tinned chicken consommé
1 ¼ teaspoons powdered gelatine
½ orange, very thinly sliced

Put the chicken livers in a bowl and pour the milk over, ensuring the livers are coated in milk. Cover and refrigerate for 1 hour. Drain the livers, discarding the milk, then rinse in cold water, drain well and pat dry with paper towels.

Melt one-third of the butter in a frying pan. Add the spring onion and sauté over medium heat for 2–3 minutes, or until softened but not brown. Add the livers and sauté over medium heat for 4–5 minutes, or until just cooked. Remove from the heat and cool a little.

Transfer the livers to a food processor and blend until very smooth. Add the remaining butter, Grand Marnier and orange juice concentrate and blend until creamy. Season to taste with sea salt and freshly ground black pepper. Pour into a 1.25 litre (44 fl oz/5 cup) serving dish, cover the surface with plastic wrap and refrigerate for 1 ½ hours, or until firm.

To make the jelly, whisk together the orange juice concentrate, Grand Marnier and 80 ml (2 ½ fl oz/⅓ cup) of the consommé in a pouring jug. Sprinkle the gelatine over the liquid in an even layer and leave until the gelatine has softened — do not stir.

Heat the remaining consommé in a saucepan, remove from the heat and add the gelatine mixture. Stir to dissolve the gelatine, then leave until cooled and just beginning to set.

Press the orange slices lightly into the surface of the pâté and gently pour the jelly evenly over the top. Refrigerate for 1 hour, or until set. Serve at room temperature with toasted bread or a baguette loaf.

Kidneys in sherry

Serves 4–6

2 tablespoons olive oil
1 large onion, finely chopped
2 garlic cloves, crushed
1 tablespoon plain (all-purpose) flour
310 ml (10¾ fl oz/1¼ cups) chicken stock
1 tablespoon tomato paste (concentrated purée)
1 bay leaf
1 kg (2 lb 4 oz) lamb kidneys
40 g (1½ oz) clarified butter
150 ml (5 fl oz) dry sherry
1 tablespoon chopped flat-leaf (Italian) parsley

Heat the olive oil in a frying pan and sauté the onion and garlic over medium heat for 5 minutes, or until the onion has softened. Add the flour and stir for 1 minute, then add the stock, tomato paste and bay leaf. Bring the mixture to the boil and reduce the heat to low. Cook for 7–8 minutes, or until thickened and smooth, stirring often to prevent lumps forming. Season to taste with sea salt and freshly ground black pepper and simmer for a further 3–4 minutes. Set the sauce aside and keep warm.

Meanwhile, cut the kidneys in half lengthways, then trim them, removing the cores. Slice each half into three pieces.

Melt the butter in a large frying pan and add half the kidneys. Cook over high heat for 3 minutes, turning to brown all over. Remove from the pan and keep warm. Brown the remaining kidneys in the same way; remove and keep warm.

Pour the sherry into the pan and cook over high heat, stirring to loosen any bits stuck to the bottom of the pan. Cook until reduced by half. Return the kidneys to the pan, add the sauce and stir in the parsley. Season to taste with sea salt and freshly ground black pepper and simmer for another 2 minutes before serving.

Bollito misto

Serves 8

1 cotechino sausage (see Note), about 800 g (1 lb 12 oz)
1 small beef tongue, about 1.25 kg (2 lb 12 oz)
3 parsley sprigs
4 baby carrots, trimmed (keep a little of the green tops on)
1 celery stalk, sliced
2 onions, roughly chopped
10 black peppercorns
2 bay leaves
1 teaspoon sea salt
1.25 kg (2 lb 12 oz) piece of beef brisket
1 tablespoon tomato paste (concentrated purée)
1 small chicken, about 900 g (2 lb)
12 whole baby turnips, trimmed
18 baby onions, peeled and trimmed
mustard fruits, to serve

SALSA VERDE
6 anchovy fillets, drained
1 ½ tablespoons capers, drained
2 garlic cloves, crushed
a large handful of flat-leaf (Italian) parsley
a large handful of basil
a large handful of mint
3 teaspoons red wine vinegar
4 tablespoons extra virgin olive oil
1 ½ teaspoons dijon mustard

Using the tip of a small, sharp knife, prick the cotechino sausage several times. Place in a saucepan and cover with cold water. Slowly bring to the boil, then reduce the heat, cover and simmer for 1 ½ hours, or until tender. Leave the sausage in the cooking liquid until ready to use.

Meanwhile, bring a stockpot or very large saucepan of water to the boil. Add the tongue, parsley sprigs, carrots, celery, onion, peppercorns, bay leaves and sea salt. Bring back to the boil, skimming off any scum that rises to the surface, then add the beef brisket and tomato paste. Cover the pot, reduce the heat and simmer for 2 hours, skimming the surface from time to time.

Add the chicken, turnips and baby onions and simmer for a further 1 hour, adding extra boiling water if necessary; the meat should always be just covered. Add the cotechino sausage for the last 20 minutes of cooking.

Meanwhile, make the salsa verde. Put the anchovies, capers, garlic, parsley, basil and mint in a food processor and chop in short bursts until roughly blended. Transfer to a bowl and stir in the vinegar. Slowly mix in the olive oil, then the mustard. Season to taste with sea salt and freshly ground black pepper and set aside.

Remove the tongue from the stockpot and take the pot off the heat. Peel the skin off the tongue, using a small knife if necessary, then trim off any gristle or tough pieces. Cut into slices and arrange on a warmed platter. Slice the cotechino sausage and beef, and cut the chicken into quarters. Arrange all the meats on the platter, then add the drained carrots, turnips and onions. Moisten with a little of the cooking liquid and serve with the salsa verde and mustard fruits.

NOTE: Cotechino sausage is a large, sweet-tasting boiling sausage from the north of Italy, made from pork (including a bit of skin to make it gelatinous). You will need to buy it from an Italian butcher.

If you are lucky enough to find a zampone (pork sausage stuffed into a pig's trotter), use it instead of the cotechino. You will only need a little of the cooking liquid for serving — keep the rest for making soup.

Beef cheek, olive and red onion pies

Makes 24

FILLING
2 tablespoons olive oil
500 g (1 lb 2 oz) trimmed beef cheeks (have your butcher do this), cut into 1.5 cm (5/8 inch) chunks
1 onion, finely chopped
50 g (1 3/4 oz) pancetta, finely chopped
2 garlic cloves, crushed
1 tablespoon tomato paste (concentrated purée)
250 ml (9 fl oz/1 cup) red wine
125 ml (4 fl oz/1/2 cup) beef stock
125 g (4 1/2 oz/1/2 cup) tomato passata (puréed tomatoes)
1 teaspoon dried oregano
85 g (3 oz/1/2 cup) pitted green olives, roughly chopped

750 g (1 lb 10 oz) ready-made shortcrust pastry
1 egg, lightly beaten

To make the filling, heat half the olive oil in a large saucepan and cook the beef cheeks in batches over high heat for 5 minutes, turning to brown all over. Remove and set aside.

Reduce the heat to medium–low, add the remaining oil and cook the onion, pancetta and garlic for 3–4 minutes, or until the onion has softened. Return the beef cheeks to the pan, stir in the remaining filling ingredients, then cover and simmer over low heat for 50–60 minutes, or until the cheeks are tender. Season to taste with sea salt and freshly ground black pepper. Remove the lid and cook for a further 30 minutes, or until the sauce has reduced. Set aside to cool.

Preheat the oven to 180°C (350°F/Gas 4) and place a baking tray in the oven. Grease 24 patty pans or mini muffin holes (they will need to measure about 5 cm/2 inches across the top).

Roll the pastry thinly and cut out 24 squares measuring 10 cm (4 inches) across. Repeat with a 5.5 cm (2 1/4 inch) round cutter. Fit the squares in each hole and fill with the cooled filling. Dampen the edges of the small rounds and place them over the filling to seal the pies. Using a small, sharp knife, trim away the excess pastry to make a neat round. Brush the tops with beaten egg and cut two or three slits in the top of each.

Place the pies on the hot baking tray and bake for 25 minutes, or until golden. Allow to cool slightly before removing from the tin.

Steak and kidney pudding

Serves 4

melted butter, for greasing
340 g (12 oz/2¾ cups) self-raising flour
150 g (5½ oz) butter, frozen and grated
700 g (1 lb 9 oz) chuck steak, cut into cubes
200 g (7 oz) ox kidney, cut into cubes
1 small onion, finely chopped
2 teaspoons chopped parsley
1 tablespoon plain (all-purpose) flour
1 teaspoon worcestershire sauce
185 ml (6 fl oz/¾ cup) beef stock

Grease a 1.5 litre (52 fl oz/6 cup) pudding basin (mould) with melted butter, then place a round of baking paper in the base. Place the basin in a large saucepan on a trivet or upturned saucer and pour in enough cold water to come halfway up the side of the basin. Remove the basin and bring the water to the boil, then reduce the heat so the water is simmering. Cover with a lid.

Sift the self-raising flour into a bowl and add the grated butter and a pinch of salt. Mix together with a flat-bladed knife, then add enough iced water to form a soft dough.

Reserve one-third of the dough and roll the rest out to a circle about 1 cm (½ inch) thick, dusting with flour as needed. Ease the pastry into the pudding basin, pleating and tucking as you go, and leaving a little pastry hanging over the edge. Brush out any excess flour.

Mix the steak, kidney, onion, parsley and plain flour together in a bowl. Season with sea salt and freshly ground black pepper and add the worcestershire sauce. Spoon the mixture into the pastry case, then pour in enough stock to come three-quarters of the way up the filling.

Roll out the remaining pastry into a circle large enough to cover the pudding. Fold the overhanging pastry lining the basin over the filling, then dampen the edge with water. Place the pastry circle on top of the pudding and press the edges together to seal.

Lay a sheet of foil, then a sheet of baking paper, on a work surface, and make a large pleat in the middle. Grease with melted butter and place, paper side down, across the top of the basin. Tie kitchen string securely around the rim and over the top of the basin to make a handle for lifting the pudding.

Lower the basin into the simmering water and cover with a tight-fitting lid. Simmer for 5 hours, checking every hour and topping up with boiling water as needed. Serve the pudding hot, spooned directly from the basin.

Pappardelle with sage and chicken giblet sauce

Serves 4–6

750 g (1 lb 10 oz) chicken gizzards and hearts
40 g (1 ½ oz) unsalted butter, plus extra, for tossing through the pasta
2 onions, finely chopped
2 celery stalks, finely chopped
2 carrots, finely chopped
4 garlic cloves, very thinly sliced
4 anchovies, rinsed and chopped
3 tablespoons currants
3 tablespoons tomato paste (concentrated purée)
1 tablespoon finely chopped sage
375 ml (13 fl oz/1 ½ cups) dry marsala
750 ml (26 fl oz/3 cups) chicken stock, approximately
3 tablespoons good-quality balsamic vinegar
850 g (1 lb 14 oz) fresh pappardelle pasta
3 tablespoons chopped flat-leaf parsley
grated parmesan cheese, to serve

To prepare the chicken gizzards, remove any visible fat. Cut through the flesh, taking care not to cut all the way through to the middle or you will burst the gravel sac, then pull the flesh away from the gravel sac and remove the sac. Discard the sac and cut away any hard membranes from inside the gizzards. To prepare the hearts, cut off any visible fat and any hard membranes. Roughly chop all the giblets and set aside.

Melt the butter in a large saucepan and add the onion, celery, carrot and garlic. Sauté over medium heat for 10 minutes, or until the vegetables are very soft.

Add the anchovies, currants, tomato paste, chicken giblets and sage and stir for a few minutes to combine. Pour in the marsala, stock and vinegar, adding a little extra stock to just cover the giblets if necessary. Bring the mixture to a simmer, then cook over medium–low heat for 1–1 ½ hours, or until the giblets are tender and the liquid has reduced.

Using a slotted spoon, remove the giblets from the sauce and allow to cool slightly. Finely chop using a large, sharp knife, then return to the saucepan. Season to taste with sea salt and freshly ground black pepper and gently reheat, simmering for a while to further reduce the sauce if necessary.

Meanwhile, cook the pasta in a saucepan of boiling salted water for 3 minutes, or until *al dente*. Drain well and add a few knobs of butter, tossing to coat.

Divide the pasta among six bowls, ladle the pasta sauce over, scatter with the parsley and parmesan and serve.

Ox tongue and quince tagine

Serves 6

1 ox tongue (about 1.25 kg/2 lb 12 oz), soaked for 2 hours in cold water
2 carrots, roughly chopped
2 celery stalks, roughly chopped
4 large onions, cut into 2 cm (3/4 inch) chunks
40 g (1 1/2 oz) butter
2 small quinces (about 500 g/1 lb 2 oz), peeled, cored and cut into eighths
3 tablespoons olive oil
2 teaspoons paprika
2 teaspoons ground coriander
1/2 teaspoon ground ginger
1/2 teaspoon cayenne pepper, or to taste
1/2 teaspoon powdered saffron
1 cinnamon stick
1.25 litres (44 fl oz/5 cups) chicken stock, approximately
150 g (5 1/2 oz/heaped 3/4 cup) dried apricots
4 tablespoons honey
2 1/2 tablespoons lemon juice, or to taste
a large handful of roughly chopped coriander (cilantro), plus extra sprigs, to garnish
steamed couscous or rice, to serve

Drain the tongue, rinse well, then place in a large saucepan with the carrot, celery and half the onion. Add enough cold water to cover the tongue, then slowly bring to the boil, skimming off any scum that rises to the surface. Reduce the heat and simmer for 30 minutes.

Remove the tongue, discarding the vegetables and liquid, and leave until cool enough to handle. Peel the skin off the warm tongue, using a small knife if necessary, then trim off any gristle or tough pieces and cut the tongue into 2.5 cm (1 inch) chunks. Set aside.

Melt the butter in a heavy-based frying pan. Add the quince and sauté over medium heat for 15 minutes, or until lightly golden. Set aside.

Heat the olive oil in a heavy-based saucepan, add the remaining onion and sauté over medium heat for 5 minutes, or until beginning to soften. Add the ground spices and cinnamon stick and stir for 1–2 minutes, or until fragrant. Add the stock and tongue, adding a little more stock (or water) to cover if necessary. Bring to the boil, then reduce the heat, cover and simmer for 1 hour.

Add the quince, apricots and honey, then cook for a further 30–60 minutes, or until the tongue is tender. Season to taste with sea salt and freshly ground black pepper, then stir in the lemon juice and coriander. Serve with steamed couscous or rice, garnished with coriander sprigs.

Veal sweetbreads on spinach and hazelnut salad

Serves 4

- 4 veal sweetbreads, about 200 g (7 oz) each
- 1/2 small onion
- 1 small carrot, chopped
- 1 bay leaf
- 1 clove
- 6 black peppercorns
- 1 thyme sprig
- 500 ml (17 fl oz/2 cups) veal or chicken stock
- 125 ml (4 fl oz/ 1/2 cup) dry madeira
- 125 ml (4 fl oz/ 1/2 cup) dry white wine
- seasoned plain (all-purpose) flour, for dusting
- 40 g (1 1/2 oz) clarified butter
- 1 leek, white part only, rinsed well and chopped
- 2 garlic cloves, chopped

SPINACH AND HAZELNUT SALAD

- 2 tablespoons hazelnut oil
- 1–2 tablespoons lemon juice
- 150 g (5 1/2 oz/3 1/3 cups) baby English spinach leaves
- 50 g (1 3/4 oz/ 1/3 cup) roasted hazelnut halves, skins removed, then roughly chopped

Soak the sweetbreads in cold water in the refrigerator for 3 hours, changing the water several times.

Drain the sweetbreads and place in a large saucepan with the onion, carrot, bay leaf, clove, peppercorns and thyme sprig. Cover with cold water, then slowly bring to a simmer. Simmer the sweetbreads for 2 minutes, then drain and rinse under cold running water until cool.

Remove as much of the outside membrane as possible from the sweetbreads, taking care not to damage the delicate flesh. Trim the sweetbreads, discarding any tubes or gristle. Place the sweetbreads between two plates and sit several tins of food on top to weigh them down. Refrigerate for 2 hours, then slice each piece in half lengthways to give eight pieces.

Combine the stock, madeira and wine in a saucepan and boil until reduced by half. Set aside.

Pat the sweetbreads dry with paper towels and lightly dust with the seasoned flour, shaking off the excess.

Melt 30 g (1 oz) of the butter in a large frying pan and cook the sweetbreads over medium–high heat for 3–4 minutes on each side, or until browned. Remove from the pan and keep warm.

Add the leek and garlic to the pan and sauté for 2–3 minutes, or until softened. Pour in the reduced stock mixture, stirring to loosen any bits stuck to the bottom of the pan, then boil for 5 minutes, or until reduced to 250 ml (9 fl oz/1 cup). Whisk in the remaining butter and strain the sauce through a fine sieve.

Next, make the spinach and hazelnut salad. Whisk together the hazelnut oil and lemon juice to make a dressing. Place the spinach in a bowl, pour the dressing over, season with sea salt and freshly cracked black pepper and toss until combined.

Divide the salad among four plates, top with the sweetbreads and drizzle with the sauce. Sprinkle with the roasted hazelnuts, season again and serve.

Tripe with tomatoes, mint and parmesan

Serves 4–6

1 kg (2 lb 4 oz) honeycomb tripe
2 tablespoons olive oil
250 g (8 oz) speck or streaky bacon, finely diced
2 onions, sliced
1 carrot, finely diced
1 celery stalk, thinly sliced
2 garlic cloves, crushed
400 g (14 oz) tin chopped tomatoes
500 ml (17 fl oz/2 cups) beef stock
2 bay leaves
1 rosemary sprig
2 teaspoons finely grated lemon zest
1 teaspoon balsamic vinegar
4 tablespoons chopped flat-leaf (Italian) parsley
4 tablespoons chopped mint
75 g (2½ oz/¾ cup) grated parmesan cheese

Place the tripe in a large saucepan and cover with cold water. Bring to the boil over medium heat, then remove from the heat and drain. When cool enough to handle, slice into 1 cm (½ inch) lengths.

Heat 1 tablespoon of the olive oil in a large frying pan and cook the speck over medium heat for 4 minutes, stirring occasionally. Using a slotted spoon, remove from the pan.

Heat the remaining oil in the pan, then add the onion, carrot, celery and garlic. Sauté for 5–7 minutes, or until the onion is lightly golden. Add the tripe and cook, stirring, for 2–3 minutes, or until the tripe is coloured slightly. Transfer to a large saucepan and add the tomato, stock, bay leaves, rosemary and lemon zest. Season well with freshly cracked black pepper.

Bring the mixture to a simmer over medium heat, then cover, reduce the heat and cook gently for 30 minutes.

Remove the lid and cook for a further 30 minutes, or until the sauce has reduced and thickened and the tripe is tender. Just before serving, stir in the vinegar. Divide among warmed bowls and sprinkle with the herbs and parmesan.

CRUMBED BRAINS WITH RADICCHIO, PEAR AND GINGER SALAD

SERVES 4

4 sets of lamb's brains
2 tablespoons plain (all-purpose) flour
1 egg
2 tablespoons milk
50 g (1 3/4 oz/1/2 cup) dry breadcrumbs
light olive oil, for pan-frying

RADICCHIO, PEAR AND GINGER SALAD
1 radicchio lettuce
1 baby frisée (curly endive)
3 oranges
1/2 small red onion, thinly sliced
2 corella pears, cut into wedges, core removed
3 tablespoons extra virgin olive oil
1 teaspoon red wine vinegar
a pinch of ground cinnamon
2 tablespoons orange juice
2 tablespoons very finely chopped glacé ginger, plus 2 teaspoons of the syrup

Rinse the brains under cold running water and carefully remove as much of the surrounding membrane and blood vessels as possible. Place the brains in a saucepan of lightly salted water and bring to the boil. Reduce the heat and simmer for 6–7 minutes. Drain, then plunge into a bowl of iced water. Drain again and pat dry with paper towels. If desired, cut each set through the centre horizontally to give two pieces.

Put the flour on a sheet of baking paper and season with sea salt and freshly ground black pepper. Beat the egg in a small bowl, then mix in the milk. Place the breadcrumbs in a shallow bowl.

Toss the brains in the flour, shaking off any excess. Dip them into the egg mixture, then coat with the breadcrumbs, shaking off the excess. Cover and refrigerate for 30 minutes before cooking.

Meanwhile, make the salad. Discard any tough outer radicchio and frisée leaves, thoroughly wash and dry the rest, then tear into bite-sized pieces and place in a salad bowl.

Using a small, sharp knife, peel the oranges, removing all the white pith. Cutting between the membranes and holding the oranges over a bowl to catch the juices, remove the orange segments. Add them to the salad leaves with the onion and pears.

Whisk the olive oil, vinegar, cinnamon, orange juice, ginger and ginger syrup in a small bowl. Season to taste with sea salt and freshly ground black pepper and set aside. Just before serving, pour the dressing over the salad and lightly toss.

Heat some olive oil in a heavy-based frying pan. Add the brains and cook over medium heat for 6–8 minutes, or until golden brown on all sides. Remove and drain on paper towels. Serve hot, with the salad.

NOTE: This salad is also lovely using figs instead of pears, when in season. You'll need 8 small green figs, cut into quarters.

Venetian liver

Serves 4

- 2 tablespoons olive oil
- 60 g (2¼ oz) butter
- 2 large onions, cut in half and thinly sliced
- 600 g (1 lb 5 oz) calf's liver, membrane removed, trimmed and thinly sliced
- 1 tablespoon finely chopped parsley
- lemon wedges, to serve

Heat the olive oil and half the butter in a large frying pan. Add the onion, then cover and cook over low heat, stirring occasionally, for 30–40 minutes, or until very soft and golden. Season well with sea salt and freshly ground black pepper and transfer to a bowl.

Melt the remaining butter in the frying pan. Increase the heat to medium–high. Add the liver slices and cook for 10–15 seconds, or until lightly browned, turning often.

Return the onion to the pan and cook, stirring often, for a further 1–2 minutes, or until the liver is just cooked — it should still be pink in the middle. Remove from the heat, stir in the parsley and check for seasoning. Serve hot, with lemon wedges.

Braised oxtail

Serves 6

3 tablespoons extra virgin olive oil
16 small oxtail pieces, about 1.5 kg (3 lb 5 oz) in total
4 baby potatoes, cut in half
1 large onion, chopped
2 carrots, chopped
250 g (9 oz) button mushrooms
2 tablespoons plain (all-purpose) flour
750 ml (26 fl oz/3 cups) beef stock
1 teaspoon dried marjoram
2 tablespoons worcestershire sauce

Preheat the oven to 180°C (350°F/Gas 4). Heat 2 tablespoons of the olive oil in a large, heavy-based frying pan. Add the oxtail in batches and cook over medium–high heat for about 5 minutes, turning to brown all over. Transfer to a deep casserole dish and add the potatoes.

Heat the remaining oil in the frying pan. Add the onion and carrot and sauté over medium heat for 5 minutes, or until the onion has softened. Transfer to the casserole dish.

Add the mushrooms to the frying pan, with a little more oil if necessary, and sauté over medium heat for 5 minutes. Stir in the flour, reduce the heat to low and stir for 2 minutes. Season with sea salt and freshly ground black pepper, then gradually add the stock, stirring until the liquid boils and thickens. Stir in the marjoram and worcestershire sauce, then pour the mixture over the ingredients in the casserole dish.

Cover and bake for 1½ hours. Remove the lid, stir well and cook, uncovered, for a further 30 minutes, or until the meat is very tender.

poultry

'Poultry is for the cook what canvas is for the painter,' the French gourmand Jean Anthelme Brillat-Savarin once declared. From spectacular, whole roasted birds to chopped-up sandwich fillings, and from elegant boned, stuffed breast meat to grilled legs eaten out of hand, birds bred for the table offer myriad cooking possibilities and can be served every which way.

Technically there are two types of poultry: the galliformes, which include chickens and turkeys, and anseriformes, which are waterfowl and include ducks and geese. Such birds have been reared since way back — there is evidence that the ancient Mesopotamians and Egyptians bred ducks, Germanic people were breeding geese by 1000 B.C.E., and by the time the Spanish reached South America the Aztecs had long been rearing turkeys.

How poultry is raised

In times past, chicken was more valued for its regular supply of eggs than its meat, and was consumed only on special occasions. Over the last half-century, poultry consumption in the developed world, particularly that of chicken, has sky-rocketed. Chicken-rearing has moved from paddocks and outdoor coops into large, covered sheds and barns in which tens of thousands of chickens can be raised in minimal space. Chicken meat has become so much cheaper because the birds have been bred to gain weight speedily and are fed commercial formulations that are more efficiently converted to meat.

Many modern chickens are raised in deplorable conditions. Naturally, producers stress the picture is perhaps not always as grim as some would have us believe — for example, the use of hormonal growth stimulants has been globally banned for some 40 years, even though many chickens are persistently marketed as 'hormone free'.

As with all types of meat, it is important to realise how our poultry is obtained — and what alternatives exist. The vast majority of poultry is intensively raised indoors. Most chickens live their brief lives in sheds, in a living area that, by the time they are fully fattened, equates to a page from a telephone directory, on a layer of litter that is generally not replaced during their lives. Their life cycle is around six weeks. Free-range birds take around three times as long to reach the same weight. Intensively farmed chickens can suffer bone development abnormalities; chickens with 'hock burns' are not an unusual sight at the supermarket — these are burns on the knees from kneeling in their own waste. They also experience considerable stress during 'harvesting', and a percentage die of illness long before slaughter.

Even regardless of the pain, fright and boredom they endure, these bigger, cheaper birds, it must be said, yield bland, pallid meat.

The scenario for other types of poultry isn't much better. Ducks, by nature aquatic birds, are also subject to intensive indoor farming practices, although not on the same scale. The realities of intensive turkey farming are equally bleak. Birds that should take 24 weeks to reach a mature slaughter weight are bred to maturity in dimly lit, crowded sheds in just 12–14 weeks. The turkeys are mostly Broad Breasted White, a species that are unnaturally big-breasted, but utterly disappointing in their flavour and texture.

The use of antibiotics is also widespread, which can result in certain food-borne bacteria (such as campylobacter) becoming resistant to the drugs and contaminating the meat.

Free range, organic, corn-fed?

Many consumers are turning towards birds that have been raised more thoughtfully — and taste far better too. However, the terms 'free range' and 'organic' can be hazy. While 'free range' implies the birds have had free run outdoors and are at liberty to eat from a varied diet, this is not necessarily so. In the United States, 'free range' simply means 'the poultry has been allowed access to the outside' — which could be for as little as 5 minutes per day; in some cases living conditions are very similar to those of other industrially raised birds. In the United Kingdom, a free-range chicken 'must have daytime access to open-air runs during at least half their life'. In the European Union, 'free range' birds are housed in barns, but must have continuous daylight access to outdoor runs. Also, in most countries, for a bird to be truly 'free range' it must not be subject to routine antibiotic dosing.

Generally, 'organic' poultry is the best option, but do learn about the producer and their practices. With corporations cashing in on the organic bandwagon, be sure you're getting what you think you are paying for.

'Corn fed' chickens have eaten predominantly corn all their lives, and this turns their skin and fat a distinctive yellow colour. The world's most famous corn-fed chicken is the French Poulet de Bresse, so highly regarded that it is protected by its own appellation.

Storing poultry

Small young birds such as Cornish game hens or poussin won't keep as long as older birds — use them within one or two days. Fresh chicken, duck and turkey will last for up to four days in the refrigerator if taken from its plastic wrapping. Place it on a plate or in a ceramic or glass bowl and cover with plastic wrap. Frozen poultry is best used within two months — always defrost it under refrigeration and ensure it is completely thawed before cooking it. A frozen turkey can take two days to thaw completely in the refrigerator.

CHICKEN

There are dozens and dozens of chicken varieties. Enthusiasts around the world keep flocks of heritage breeds, many of which have rather exotic characteristics. The varieties mainly in use for commercial purposes (for meat at least) are derived from the deep-breasted Cornish breed.

Cuts of chicken

A chicken has two breasts, which can be left intact and sold as a 'double' breast, or separated into single breasts. They can be cooked on or off the bone. A single breast, boneless except for the first joint of the wing, is called the 'supreme' and is used in chicken kiev. Often, breasts are sold minus their skin, but if you plan to roast, grill or barbecue them, buy ones with the skin on.

The dark leg meat, still on the bone, is full-flavoured and suited to roasting, barbecuing or braising. Legs take well to marinating or being seasoned with strong-flavoured pastes and dry rubs — make deep slashes in the meat with a sharp knife first so the flavour can penetrate.

Thighs are sold on or off the bone and are another robust-flavoured cut. With their skin on, they are excellent for braises, grilling and barbecuing; with the bone still in they are also good for roasting. Chicken leg quarters (the thigh with the leg still attached; sometimes also called a 'maryland') are sold with the skin on and can be roasted, barbecued or braised.

When trimmed down to their thickest part, chicken wings form a neat, nibble-sized cut, perfect for cocktail party or other snack-type food; they can be fried, roasted or barbecued.

Jointing a chicken

Many recipes call for chicken pieces, and although they are convenient to buy, it is more economical to cut up a chicken yourself — you'll know exactly what you are getting and you can freeze the bones and off-cuts for a large pot of stock. Jointing a chicken isn't difficult — you just need a solid chopping board and a good, heavy, sharp knife or poultry shears. See the jointing instructions in the *coq au vin* recipe on page 200.

Roasting chicken

This is the classic preparation for a whole chicken — and so simple to do. It is important though to find the freshest, best-quality chicken your money will buy and bring it to cool room temperature before roasting. See the roasted chicken recipes on page 194 and 203 for more specific directions.

An instant-read, digital thermometer will register 180°C (350°F) when the bird is cooked. Always rest the bird for 10 minutes before carving.

Grilling or barbecuing

Chicken is excellent barbecued or grilled, especially pieces cooked on the bone with the skin on to protect the meat from drying out. The trick is to regulate the temperature so that the skin doesn't burn while the meat cooks. Keep the meat about 10 cm (4 inches) away from the heat source.

If cooking a whole bird, a half, or a large piece such as a breast or leg quarter, cook it skin side down for two-thirds of the total cooking time, and the flesh side for the remainder, so the meat doesn't dry out. A whole bird should cook in around 45 minutes, while small pieces such as wings or drumsticks will take around 15 minutes. Breast meat will need regular basting with oil or a marinade while cooking or it will dry out.

For juicy results, rest the cooked meat for 10 minutes before serving.

Braising and stewing

The classic chicken braise of all time is the French *coq au vin* (see page 200). Any chicken is good for braising or stewing — but older, larger, tougher birds have more flavour. Use pieces on the bone with the skin still on (such as legs and thighs) — the flavour will be better and the dish will have more body.

Brown the pieces first, then cover with the braising liquid and slowly simmer until the meat is very tender and almost falling off the bone. Breast pieces will braise more quickly than other cuts, so remove them when they are done and reheat just before serving. The braising liquid should be well-skimmed of fat — it may also need to be strained and boiled to reduce and thicken before being served with the chicken. A braised dish always tastes better the next day when the flavours have developed.

Chicken is wonderful braised with tomato-based sauces and flavours such as capers, olives, oregano and prosciutto... or even with cider, apples and potatoes, finished with a dash of cream. Mustard and tarragon, prunes, rosemary and dried beans, and lemon and egg yolks (to thicken the braising liquid) are also good. The tagines and other spicy stews from North Africa, India and Asia attest to its compatibility with aromatic spices, acidic touches like preserved lemons and lime juice, and nuts such as almonds and walnuts.

POACHING

Poaching chicken (a whole bird, or breasts) yields incredibly tender, mild-tasting meat (an example is the French *poulet au pot*; see page 199). The trick is to keep the liquid at just below boiling point — 'a boiling that does not boil', in the words of the great French chef Auguste Escoffier. If allowed to boil, chicken meat will become tough, dry and stringy.

Also, you need a deep saucepan just large enough to accommodate the bird. Cover the bird with cold liquid, add your vegetables and aromatics, then bring very slowly up to a simmer, skimming any scum that rises to the surface. Just as bubbles are about to break the surface, reduce the heat so the liquid stays at a bare tremble — you will need to check and adjust the heat regularly. A whole bird will cook in about an hour. The cooking liquid can be skimmed, strained and served as a broth, or kept and used for stock.

Poached chicken is excellent served with a creamy sauce or even home-made mayonnaise (flavoured with tarragon, dill, dijon mustard, garlic, chopped olives, chopped sun-dried tomatoes or lemon) spooned over.

TURKEY

The turkey is a member of the pheasant family. Once, like many of our meats, a turkey dinner was a rare treat, reserved for special occasions such as Christmas or, in the United States, Thanksgiving. Today, in the United States, some 260 million turkeys are processed each year.

The meat of intensively farmed turkeys is famously dry and bland. Producers pump water, salt, fats and flavourings into the meat (especially the breast) to improve its taste and texture — such birds are often labelled 'self-basting' or 'pre-basted'. Mercifully, there is a marked swing back towards organic or at least free-range turkeys — and, in America, to 'heritage' breeds, which were in danger of disappearing entirely. After the insipid mildness of factory-farmed turkeys, the taste of a traditionally reared one is a revelation. Please do your utmost to shun mass-produced birds in favour of the alternatives.

Roasting turkey

Turkeys are mostly sold as whole birds, which are most popularly roasted. Large producers also sell minced (ground) turkey, drumsticks, breasts, fillets and escalopes, but unless you are happy to eat mass-produced turkey, these cuts are best avoided unless you know they are from an organic producer.

When roasting turkey, it is common to stuff the large cavity first; remove the wishbone so it will be easier to carve the breast. It is also helpful to truss the turkey — closing the rear-end cavity and pinning the wings and legs close to the body, which gives a neat shape and ensures the bird cooks through more evenly. All birds benefit from trussing. With a smaller bird, such as a chicken, you can simply tie the legs together with kitchen string, but with a turkey, you need a special trussing needle.

To stop the turkey breast drying out during roasting, slices of fatty bacon or pancetta can be wrapped over it; you can also cover it with foil.

If fast-roasting a whole turkey, rub the bird well with olive oil or butter, then season and place in a large roasting dish. Roast in a 220°C (425°F/Gas 7) oven for 45 minutes. Reduce the oven temperature to 180°C (350°F/Gas 4) until the bird is just cooked — the juices should run clear when the tip of a sharp knife (or metal skewer) is inserted into the joint between the body and the thigh (the thickest part of the bird). During roasting, turn the bird onto each side, and also breast side down, for equal amounts of time. As an approximate guide, a 5.5–7 kg (12–15 lb) turkey will take about 2 hours to fast roast, and a 7–9 kg (15–20 lb) bird around 2¾ hours.

To slow-roast a turkey, simply leave it in a 170°C (325°F/Gas 3) oven, turning it and covering the breast as before. A 5.5–7 kg (12–15 lb) bird will take about 4 hours to cook, and a 7–9 kg (15–20 lb) up to 5 hours.

Always rest the bird for at least 30 minutes before carving.

DUCK

Although 'red' in colour, duck meat is technically a white meat. As a flying bird, the breast muscles have more oxygen-delivering red blood cells than those of chickens, hence their dark colour. Ducks also have a thick layer of breast fat and smaller, thinner breasts. Duck is more expensive than chicken and is often perceived as bad value: a whole bird weighing around 1.8 kg (4 lb) will feed only two or three. But duck — good, meaty, juicy duck — is wonderfully delicious and deserves a special spot at the dining table.

Duck can be purchased as a whole bird, breasts, and whole duck legs (with the thighs still attached). A whole duck is commonly roasted, the breasts are best grilled, barbecued or roasted, and the legs make fabulous braises, rillettes or, most famously, confit (see page 219).

Roasting a whole duck

When a duck is roasted, much of the fat layer on the breast renders out and helps keep the meat moist. The fat gives the slightly gamey taste of duck a certain richness, making it a great partner for sweet and acidic flavours. Classic combinations are duck with orange, cherries, raspberries or slightly vinegary braised red cabbage; it also teams beautifully with assertive flavours such as honey, ginger, olives, garlic, anchovies, radish and turnips.

To roast a duck, give it a good wipe, rub the skin well with olive oil, then season and place, breast side down, in a roasting pan. Roast in a 220°C (425°F/Gas 7) oven for 20 minutes, then reduce the oven temperature to 180°C (350°F/Gas 4). Pour off the fat, turn the duck on its side and cook for another 60–70 minutes, turning it to the other side and pouring off the fat again about halfway through. Cover the breast with foil if it is cooking too quickly. The cooking time will depend on its size, but the juices should still run a little pink when the duck is pierced with a skewer between the leg and the body — the duck is at its juicy best when the meat is on the pink side of cooked. Rest the duck for 20 minutes or so before carving.

If you prefer, carve the breasts from the roast when they are just cooked but still a little pink; rest them, covered, for 10 minutes and serve sliced and tossed in a salad as an entrée. Continue to roast the legs until they are cooked, then serve them as a main with accompaniments of your choice.

Pan-frying

To cook duck breasts off the bone, first make some slashes through the skin (to help render out some of the fat), but not down to the flesh. Place the breasts, fat side down, in a heavy-based pan over medium–high heat. Cook for 8–10 minutes, or until the breast feels somewhat firm. Turn and brown the other side for 2 minutes. Rest for 5 minutes before serving.

Braising

Duck legs are best when braised or turned into confit. Gently braise the legs, on the bone, for 1–1½ hours in liquid spiked with red wine, tomato or orange juice, with flavours such as rosemary, olives, pancetta, thyme, juniper berries, honey and ginger. The meat can be served on the bone, or removed and shredded; the braise then makes an excellent sauce over pasta or polenta.

Chargrilled chicken with spinach and raspberries

Serves 4

2 tablespoons raspberry vinegar
2 tablespoons lime juice
2 garlic cloves, crushed
1 tablespoon chopped oregano
1 teaspoon soft brown sugar
2 small red chillies, finely chopped
3 tablespoons extra virgin olive oil
4 boneless, skinless chicken breasts
200 g (7 oz/4½ cups) baby English spinach leaves
250 g (9 oz) fresh raspberries

DRESSING
3 tablespoons extra virgin olive oil
1 tablespoon raspberry vinegar
1 tablespoon chopped oregano
1 teaspoon dijon mustard
¼ teaspoon sea salt

In a large bowl, mix together the vinegar, lime juice, garlic, oregano, sugar, chilli and olive oil. Add the chicken breasts, turning to coat, then cover and refrigerate for 2 hours.

Preheat the oven to 180°C (350°F/Gas 4).

Heat a chargrill pan or barbecue chargrill plate to medium–high. Cook the chicken for 3 minutes on each side.

Place the chicken breasts on a baking tray and bake for 5 minutes, or until just cooked through. Remove from the oven, cover loosely with foil and leave to rest in a warm place for 5 minutes. Carve each breast on the diagonal into five pieces.

Mix together the dressing ingredients and season to taste with freshly ground black pepper.

Gently toss the spinach and raspberries in a serving bowl with half the dressing. Arrange the chicken over the top and drizzle with the remaining dressing.

Chicken and egg pie

Serves 8

125 g (4½ oz/1 cup) plain (all-purpose) flour
125 g (4½ oz/1 cup) self-raising flour
150 g (5½ oz) cold butter, chopped
1 egg yolk, lightly beaten, plus extra, for glazing

FILLING
1.5 kg (3 lb 5 oz) boneless, skinless chicken thighs, trimmed and cut into 2 cm (¾ inch) pieces
200 g (7 oz) leg ham, cut off the bone, then chopped
6 spring onions (scallions), finely chopped
1 tablespoon chopped parsley
1 teaspoon mixed dried herbs
5 hard-boiled eggs

Sift all the flour into a mixing bowl. Rub the butter in with your fingertips until the mixture resembles coarse breadcrumbs. Using a fork, stir in the egg yolk and enough iced water to form a firm dough. Shape the pastry into a disc, cover with plastic wrap and refrigerate for 30 minutes.

Preheat the oven to 190°C (375°F/Gas 5). Grease a 23 cm (9 inch) spring-form tin.

Reserve one-third of the pastry and roll the rest out to fit over the base and side of the prepared tin. Line the tin with the pastry.

To make the filling, put the chicken and ham in a bowl with the spring onion, parsley and mixed herbs. Season with sea salt and freshly ground black pepper and mix together well. Spoon half the filling into the pastry case.

Shell the hard-boiled eggs. Leave them whole and arrange over the filling. Spoon the remaining filling over the top.

Roll the remaining pastry out to a circle large enough to cover the top of the pie. Moisten the pastry edges with a little extra beaten egg yolk, then place the pastry circle over, pressing the edges together to seal. Trim the edges. Cut out shapes from the pastry trimmings and use them to decorate the top of the pie, then brush with egg yolk. Cut two small slits in the top of the pie to allow steam to escape. Bake for 30 minutes.

Reduce the oven temperature to 180°C (350°F/Gas 4) and bake for a further 1 hour, covering the top of the pie with foil if the pastry browns too quickly. Remove from the oven and allow to cool completely in the tin before removing. Refrigerate until needed. Serve cut into wedges.

Chicken with Cognac and Shallots

Serves 4

- 1 tablespoon olive oil
- 30 g (1 oz) butter
- 1.8 kg (4 lb) chicken pieces, trimmed of excess fat
- 2 tablespoons Cognac or brandy
- 8 French shallots, peeled
- 2 tablespoons chicken stock
- 2 tablespoons dry white wine
- 3 thyme sprigs

Heat the olive oil and half the butter in a large frying pan over medium–high heat. Add the chicken pieces, in batches if necessary, and cook for 3–4 minutes on each side, or until browned all over. Transfer to a large flameproof casserole dish.

Place the dish over low heat and sprinkle the Cognac over the chicken. Light a match and carefully lower the flame onto the Cognac until it ignites, then allow the flame to burn until it extinguishes itself.

Melt the remaining butter in the same frying pan over medium–low heat and fry the shallots for 5 minutes, or until softened but not browned. Pour in the stock and wine, increase the heat to high and boil for 30 seconds, stirring to loosen any bits stuck to the bottom of the pan. Pour the pan contents over the chicken and add the thyme sprigs.

Cover the casserole tightly with foil to completely seal, then cover with a tight-fitting lid. Bring to a gentle simmer over very low heat and simmer for 45 minutes, or until the chicken is tender. Transfer the chicken pieces to a plate and keep warm.

Increase the heat to high, then boil the liquid in the casserole until thickened to a light coating consistency. Spoon the sauce over the chicken and serve.

Crisp chicken wings

Serves 6

12 chicken wings
3 tablespoons soy sauce
3 tablespoons hoisin sauce
125 ml (4 fl oz/½ cup) tomato sauce (ketchup)
2 tablespoons honey
1 tablespoon soft brown sugar
1 tablespoon cider vinegar
2 garlic cloves, crushed
¼ teaspoon Chinese five-spice
2 teaspoons sesame oil

Tuck the chicken wing tips to the underside of each wing and place in a non-metallic bowl.

In another bowl, mix together the remaining ingredients, then pour over the chicken wings, turning to coat. Cover and refrigerate for at least 2 hours, turning occasionally.

Drain the wings, reserving the marinade. Heat a lightly oiled barbecue grill plate, flat plate or chargrill pan to high. Cook the chicken wings for 5 minutes, or until cooked through, brushing with the reserved marinade several times during cooking.

Lebanese chicken

Serves 4–6

250 g (9 oz/1 cup) Greek-style yoghurt
2 teaspoons soft brown sugar
4 garlic cloves, crushed
3 teaspoons ground cumin
1½ teaspoons ground coriander
3 tablespoons chopped flat-leaf (Italian) parsley
3 tablespoons lemon juice
1.8 kg (4 lb) whole chicken, cut into 8 pieces (see the *coq au vin* recipe on page 200)

EGGPLANT, TOMATO AND SUMAC SALAD
2 eggplants (aubergines), cut into 1 cm (½ inch) thick rounds
100 ml (3½ fl oz) olive oil
5 large ripe tomatoes, cut into wedges
1 small red onion, finely sliced
a handful of mint, roughly chopped
a handful of flat-leaf (Italian) parsley, roughly chopped
2 teaspoons sumac (see Note)
2 tablespoons lemon juice

Put the yoghurt, sugar, garlic, ground spices, parsley and lemon juice in a large non-metallic bowl and mix together well. Add the chicken pieces, turning to coat, then cover and refrigerate for at least 2 hours, or preferably overnight.

Nearer to serving time, start preparing the eggplant, tomato and sumac salad. Put the eggplant in a colander, sprinkle with salt and leave for 1 hour. Rinse, drain well, then pat dry with paper towels.

Heat a lightly oiled barbecue grill plate, flat plate or chargrill pan to medium. Using 2 tablespoons of the olive oil, brush the eggplant slices on each side, then grill them for 5 minutes on each side, or until cooked through. Remove from the heat, allow to cool slightly and cut in half.

Drain the chicken well, then season with sea salt and freshly ground black pepper. Grill the chicken pieces, turning frequently, for 20–30 minutes, or until cooked through — the breast pieces will cook more quickly than those on the bone, so remove them as they are ready and keep warm.

Arrange the eggplant, tomato and onion in a serving bowl. Scatter the mint, parsley and sumac over the top, then put the lemon juice and remaining olive oil in a small screw-top jar, season and shake well. Drizzle the dressing over the salad and serve with the chicken.

NOTE: Sumac is a spice made from crushing the dried sumac berry. It has a mild lemony flavour and is widely used throughout the Middle East.

Chicken, artichoke and broad bean stew

Serves 4

- 60 g (2¼ oz/½ cup) plain (all-purpose) flour
- 8 chicken thighs on the bone, skin on
- 2 tablespoons olive oil
- 1 large red onion, cut into small wedges
- 125 ml (4 fl oz/½ cup) dry white wine
- 250 ml (9 fl oz/1 cup) chicken stock
- 2 teaspoons finely chopped rosemary
- 340 g (12 oz) jar of marinated artichoke hearts, drained well and cut into quarters
- 155 g (5½ oz/1 cup) frozen broad (fava) beans, peeled

POTATO MASH

- 800 g (1 lb 12 oz) potatoes, peeled and cut into large chunks
- 60 g (2¼ oz) butter
- 3 tablespoons chicken stock

Season the flour with sea salt and freshly ground black pepper. Dust the chicken thighs in the flour, shaking off the excess.

Heat the olive oil in a saucepan or flameproof casserole dish. Add the chicken in batches and brown over medium heat for 8 minutes, turning once. Remove and drain on paper towels.

Add the onion to the pan and sauté for 3–4 minutes, or until softened but not browned. Increase the heat to high, add the wine and boil for 2 minutes, or until reduced to a syrupy consistency. Stir in the stock and bring the mixture just to the boil.

Return the chicken to the pan and add the rosemary. Reduce the heat to low, then cover and simmer for 45 minutes.

Add the artichoke, increase the heat to high and return to the boil. Reduce to a simmer and cook, uncovered, for 10–15 minutes. Add the broad beans and cook for a further 5 minutes.

Meanwhile, make the potato mash. Cook the potato in a saucepan of boiling salted water for 15–20 minutes, or until tender. Drain, then return to the saucepan. Add the butter and stock and mash well using a potato masher.

Spoon the mashed potato into four warmed shallow bowls, then spoon the stew over or around and serve.

Chicken and spinach orzo soup

Serves 4

- 1 tablespoon olive oil
- 1 leek, trimmed and cut into quarters lengthways, then rinsed well and thinly sliced
- 2 garlic cloves, crushed
- 1 teaspoon ground cumin
- 1.5 litres (52 fl oz/6 cups) chicken stock
- 2 boneless, skinless chicken breasts, about 500 g (1 lb 2 oz) in total
- 200 g (7 oz/1 cup) orzo (see Note)
- 150 g (5½ oz/3 cups) baby English spinach leaves, roughly chopped
- 1 tablespoon chopped dill
- 2 teaspoons lemon juice

Heat the olive oil in a large saucepan over low heat. Add the leek and sauté for 8–10 minutes, or until soft. Add the garlic and cumin and cook for 1 minute.

Pour in the stock, increase the heat to high and bring to the boil. Reduce the heat to low, add the chicken breasts, then cover and simmer for 8 minutes. Remove the chicken, reserving the liquid (keep it covered over low heat to keep it hot). When the chicken is cool enough to handle, shred it finely using your fingers.

Stir the orzo into the simmering stock and simmer for 12 minutes, or until *al dente*.

Return the chicken to the pan and add the spinach and dill. Simmer for 2 minutes, or until the spinach has wilted. Stir in the lemon juice, season to taste with sea salt and freshly ground black pepper and serve.

NOTE: Orzo is a small rice-shaped pasta, readily available from supermarkets.

Roast chicken with herbed cheese

Serves 4

- 125 g (4½ oz/½ cup) cream cheese, chopped
- 25 g (1 oz) butter, softened
- 1 tablespoon chopped marjoram
- 1½ tablespoons chopped flat-leaf (Italian) parsley
- 1 teaspoon finely grated lemon zest
- 4 chicken leg quarters or boneless chicken breasts, with skin on
- 2 leeks, white part only, rinsed well and cut into chunks
- 2 parsnips, peeled and cut into chunks
- 2 teaspoons extra virgin olive oil

Preheat the oven to 200°C (400°F/Gas 6).

Put the cream cheese, butter, marjoram, parsley and lemon zest in a food processor. Season to taste with sea salt and freshly ground black pepper, then blend until well combined and smooth.

Using your fingers, loosen the skin from the chicken legs or breasts and spread 2 tablespoons of the cream cheese mixture between the skin and flesh of each. Smooth the skin back to its original position and season well with sea salt and freshly ground black pepper.

Cook the leek and parsnip in a saucepan of boiling, salted water for 4 minutes, then drain well. Transfer to a baking dish, arranging the vegetables in a single layer. Drizzle with the olive oil, season well, then place the chicken pieces on top. Roast for 40 minutes, or until the chicken is golden, the vegetables are tender and the cream cheese mixture is melted and bubbly. Serve hot.

Circassian chicken

Serves 6

2 teaspoons paprika
1/4 teaspoon cayenne pepper
1 tablespoon walnut oil
4 skinless chicken breasts, on the bone
4 chicken wings
1 large onion, chopped
2 celery stalks, roughly chopped
1 carrot, chopped
1 bay leaf
4 parsley sprigs
1 thyme sprig
6 black peppercorns
1 teaspoon coriander seeds

WALNUT SAUCE
250 g (9 oz) walnuts, roasted (see Note)
2 slices of white bread, crusts removed
1 tablespoon paprika
4 garlic cloves, crushed

Put the paprika and cayenne pepper in a small frying pan and dry-fry over low heat for 2 minutes, or until fragrant. Stir in the walnut oil and set aside.

Put all the chicken pieces in a large saucepan with all the vegetables, herbs and spices. Add 1 litre (35 fl oz/4 cups) water and bring to the boil, skimming off any scum that forms on the surface. Reduce the heat to low and simmer for 15–20 minutes, or until the chicken is tender. Remove the saucepan from the heat and leave the chicken to cool in the stock.

Remove the chicken to a plate and return the stock to the heat. Simmer for 20–25 minutes, or until the stock has reduced by half. Strain, skimming off any fat.

Remove the skin and bones from the chicken, then shred the flesh into bite-sized pieces into a bowl. Season well with sea salt and freshly ground black pepper and ladle a little stock over the chicken to moisten.

Next, make the walnut sauce. Reserve a few of the walnuts to garnish, then put the remaining walnuts in a food processor and chop until a coarse paste forms. Put the bread in a bowl, pour in 125 ml (4 fl oz/1/2 cup) of the warm stock, then add the bread and stock to the food processor. Using the pulse button, blend for several seconds, then add the paprika, garlic and some sea salt and freshly ground black pepper. Blend until smooth. With the motor running, slowly add 250 ml (9 fl oz/1 cup) of the warm stock, adding a little more stock if necessary, until the sauce is of a smooth, pourable consistency.

Pour half the walnut sauce over the shredded chicken, tossing to coat well, then arrange on a serving platter. Pour the remaining sauce over, then sprinkle with the reserved walnuts and spiced walnut oil. Serve at room temperature.

NOTE: Use only the freshest walnuts for this recipe as walnuts that are slightly old can be rancid, causing the dish to taste bitter. To roast walnuts, spread them on a baking tray in a single layer and bake in a 175°C (335°F/Gas 3–4) oven for 8–10 minutes.

Vinegar-poached spatchcocks

Serves 4

- 4 x 500 g (1 lb 2 oz) spatchcocks (poussin)
- 1 large carrot, chopped
- 1 large onion, chopped
- 1 celery stalk, chopped
- 1 bouquet garni
- 1 ½ tablespoons sugar
- 500 ml (17 fl oz/2 cups) white wine vinegar
- 3 tablespoons balsamic vinegar
- 1 tablespoon butter
- 1 tablespoon plain (all-purpose) flour
- 150 ml (5 fl oz) chicken stock

Trim any fat from the spatchcocks and season well, both inside and out, with sea salt and freshly ground black pepper. Using kitchen string, tie the legs together and tuck the wings behind each spatchcock.

Put the carrot, onion and celery in a flameproof casserole dish or saucepan large enough to fit the spatchcocks in a single layer. Add the bouquet garni, sugar and all the vinegar and bring to the boil. Reduce the heat to low and simmer for 5 minutes.

Place the spatchcocks on top of the vegetables, breast side up. Add enough boiling water to just cover the birds, then cover and simmer for 25 minutes, or until the birds are just cooked. Remove the dish from the heat and set aside for 10 minutes.

Melt the butter in a small saucepan. Add the flour and stir for 30 seconds. Gradually stir in the stock, then simmer until smooth and thickened. Stir in 3–4 tablespoons of the chicken poaching liquid and season to taste. Continue adding a little poaching liquid — about 125 ml (4 fl oz/½ cup) in total — until a thin sauce forms, stirring constantly to prevent lumps forming. Increase the heat and simmer for 5 minutes, then season to taste.

Remove the spatchcocks from the casserole dish, drain well and arrange on a warm serving platter. Spoon just enough sauce over the birds to glaze the skin.

Grilled marinated spatchcock with green olive gremolata

Serves 4

4 x 500 g (1 lb 2 oz) spatchcocks (poussin)
125 ml (4 fl oz/½ cup) olive oil
4 garlic cloves, crushed
2 teaspoons finely grated lemon zest
3 tablespoons lemon juice
2 tablespoons finely chopped flat-leaf (Italian) parsley, plus extra, to serve
lemon wedges, to serve

GREEN OLIVE GREMOLATA
100 g (3½ oz/¾ cup) pitted green olives, finely chopped
2 teaspoons grated lemon zest
2 garlic cloves, finely chopped

To prepare the spatchcocks, twist each thigh at the thigh joint to separate it from the body. Put the birds on a board, breast side down, and cut along the backbone from the neck to the tail end. Carefully scrape away the flesh on one side of the backbone, cutting into the birds to expose the rib cage. Repeat on the other side of the backbone, being careful not to pierce the breast skin, then remove the ribs and backbones. Scrape away the flesh from each thigh bone and cut away the bone at the joint.

In a small bowl, combine the olive oil, garlic, lemon zest, lemon juice and parsley. Place the spatchcock pieces in a large, shallow non-metallic dish, pour the oil mixture over and toss to coat well. Cover and refrigerate for 3 hours, or preferably overnight, turning occasionally.

Near serving time, put the gremolata ingredients in a small bowl, mix well, then cover and refrigerate until needed.

Heat a barbecue grill plate, chargrill plate or chargrill pan to high. Cook the spatchcock pieces for 5 minutes on each side, or until cooked through. Remove to a warmed plate, cover loosely with foil and leave to rest for 7–8 minutes.

Divide among warmed serving plates, sprinkle with some extra parsley and serve with the gremolata and lemon wedges.

Poulet au pot

Serves 4

1 large chicken, about 1.8–2 kg (4 lb–4 lb 8 oz)
3 litres (105 fl oz/12 cups) chicken stock
4 cloves
1 onion, cut into quarters
2 celery stalks, chopped
2 bay leaves
1 kg (2 lb 4 oz) small baby potatoes
12 baby carrots, trimmed
3 leeks, white part only, rinsed well and cut into 5 cm (2 inch) lengths
1 tablespoon roughly chopped flat-leaf (Italian) parsley
2 teaspoons thyme
1 teaspoon finely chopped lemon zest
dijon mustard, to serve

AÏOLI
1 garlic clove
1 egg yolk
125 ml (4 fl oz/½ cup) olive oil
2 teaspoons lemon juice

Put the chicken in a large saucepan and pour in the stock. Stud a clove into each onion quarter and add to the saucepan along with the celery and bay leaves. Bring to the boil, skimming any scum from the surface, then reduce the heat and and simmer gently for 1 hour.

Meanwhile, make the aïoli. Put the garlic and egg yolk in a food processor and blend until smooth. With the motor running, gradually add the olive oil in a thin, steady stream until the mixture thickens. Stir in the lemon juice and season to taste with sea salt and freshly ground black pepper. Cover and refrigerate until needed.

Remove the chicken to a warmed plate and cover loosely with foil. Strain the poaching liquid into a bowl, then pour it back into the saucepan and bring to the boil. Add the potatoes and carrots and cook for 10 minutes. Add the leek and cook for a further 10 minutes, or until all the vegetables are tender.

Meanwhile, carve the chicken into serving pieces and keep warm.

To serve, remove the cooked vegetables from the poaching liquid and arrange in a large serving dish. Put the chicken pieces on top and pour the hot poaching liquid over. Scatter with the parsley, thyme and lemon zest and serve with the aïoli and dijon mustard.

Coq au vin

Serves 8

2 x 1.6 kg (3 lb 8 oz) chickens
750 ml (26 fl oz/3 cups) red wine
2 bay leaves
2 thyme sprigs
250 g (9 oz) bacon, diced
60 g (2 1/4 oz) butter, plus extra, if needed
20 baby onions
250 g (9 oz) button mushrooms
1 teaspoon oil
3 tablespoons plain (all-purpose) flour, plus extra, if needed
1 litre (35 fl oz/4 cups) chicken stock
125 ml (4 fl oz/1/2 cup) brandy
2 teaspoons tomato paste (concentrated purée)
crusty bread, to serve

Cut each chicken into eight pieces by removing both legs, then cutting between the joint of the drumstick and the thigh. Cut down either side of the backbone and discard the backbone (save it for stock). Turn the chicken over and cut lengthways through the centre of the breastbone. Cut each breast in half on a slight diagonal, leaving the wing attached to the top half.

In a large bowl, mix together the wine, bay leaves and thyme with some sea salt and freshly ground black pepper. Add the chicken pieces, turning to coat, then cover and refrigerate overnight.

Cook the bacon for 1 minute in boiling water, then drain well and pat dry with paper towels. Heat a non-stick frying pan, add the bacon and cook over medium heat for 5–6 minutes, or until golden. Remove and set aside.

Melt 15 g (1/2 oz) of the butter in the same frying pan. Add the onions and sauté for 7–8 minutes, or until golden. Remove to a bowl.

Melt another 15 g (1/2 oz) of the butter in the frying pan. Add the mushrooms, season well and sauté for 5 minutes. Remove and add to the onions.

Drain the chicken pieces, reserving the marinade, and pat dry with paper towels. Season well. Add the remaining butter and the oil to the pan, add the chicken pieces in batches and cook, turning once, for 10 minutes, or until golden. Stir in the flour. Transfer the chicken and pan juices to a large saucepan or flameproof casserole dish and add the stock.

Pour the brandy into the frying pan and boil, stirring for 30 seconds to loosen any bits stuck to the bottom of the pan. Pour the brandy over the chicken. Add the marinade, onions, mushrooms, bacon and tomato paste, then simmer over medium heat for 45 minutes, or until the chicken is cooked through.

If the sauce needs thickening, remove the chicken and vegetables and bring the sauce to the boil. Mix together 1 1/2 tablespoons softened butter and 1 tablespoon plain flour and whisk into the sauce. Boil, stirring, for 2 minutes, or until thickened. Return the chicken and vegetables to the sauce and serve with crusty bread.

Roast chicken with bacon and sage stuffing

Serves 6

2 x 1.2 kg (2 lb 11 oz) chickens
4 slices of bacon
2 tablespoons olive oil
1 small onion, finely chopped
1 tablespoon chopped sage
125 g (4½ oz/1½ cups) fresh breadcrumbs
1 egg, lightly beaten

WINE GRAVY
2 tablespoons plain (all-purpose) flour
2 teaspoons worcestershire sauce
2 tablespoons red or white wine
560 ml (19¼ fl oz/2¼ cups) beef or chicken stock

Preheat the oven to 180°C (350°F/Gas 4). Wipe the chickens and pat dry with paper towels.

Finely chop half the bacon. Heat half the olive oil in a small frying pan, then add the onion and chopped bacon and sauté for 7–8 minutes over medium heat, or until the onion is soft and the bacon is starting to brown. Transfer to a bowl, allow to cool, then add the sage, breadcrumbs and egg. Mix well and season to taste with sea salt and freshly ground black pepper. Divide the mixture among the chicken cavities.

Fold the wings back and tuck them under the chickens. Tie the legs of each chicken together with kitchen string. Place the chickens on a rack in a large flameproof baking dish, making sure they are not touching, and brush with some of the remaining oil. Pour 250 ml (9 fl oz/1 cup) water into the baking dish.

Cut the remaining bacon into long, thin strips and lay them across the chicken breasts. Brush the bacon with a little more oil. Bake for 45–60 minutes, or until the juices run clear when a chicken thigh is pierced with a skewer. Remove from the oven, cover loosely with foil and leave to rest in a warm place while making the gravy.

To make the wine gravy, discard all but 2 tablespoons of the pan juices from the baking dish. Heat the dish over medium heat, stir in the flour and cook, stirring, until well browned. Remove from the heat and gradually add the worcestershire sauce, wine and stock. Return to the heat, stir until the mixture boils and thickens, then simmer for 2 minutes. Season to taste and serve with the roast chickens.

Timballo

Serves 6

6 tomatoes
2 tablespoons olive oil
1 large onion, finely chopped
2 garlic cloves, crushed
3 boneless, skinless chicken breasts, about 1 kg (2 lb 4 oz) in total
2 chicken thighs
1 bay leaf
2 thyme sprigs
3 tablespoons white wine
175 g (6 oz) button mushrooms, sliced
75 g (2½ oz/⅔ cup) provolone cheese, grated
9 eggs, beaten
2 tablespoons thick (double/heavy) cream
3 tablespoons chopped parsley
500 g (1 lb 2 oz) ziti (see Note)

Using a small, sharp knife, score a small cross in the base of each tomato. Plunge into boiling water for 20 seconds, then drain and plunge into iced water to cool. Peel the skin away from the cross, then cut the flesh into small pieces.

Heat the olive oil in a large saucepan. Add the onion and garlic and sauté over medium heat for 7 minutes, or until the onion has softened. Add the tomatoes and cook over low heat for 5 minutes. Add the chicken breasts and thighs, the bay leaf and thyme sprigs and stir well. Stir in the wine, then cover and cook over medium heat for 20 minutes. Season with sea salt and freshly ground black pepper.

Add the mushrooms and cook for a further 10–15 minutes, or until the chicken is cooked through, turning once during cooking. Remove the chicken from the saucepan and cook the sauce, uncovered, until it has reduced by about half. Remove the bay leaf and thyme sprigs and leave the sauce to cool to room temperature.

Pull the chicken meat from the bones, shred the meat and return to the sauce. Stir in the cheese, eggs, cream and parsley. Season to taste.

Preheat the oven to 180°C (350°F/Gas 4). Lightly grease a 1.5 litre (52 fl oz/6 cup) round baking dish.

Cook the pasta in a large saucepan of boiling salted water until *al dente*. Drain well. Use the pasta to line the baking dish — arrange the pasta, one piece at a time, in a single layer, starting in the middle of the base, then working outwards to completely cover the base and side. Make sure there are no gaps.

Fill the dish with the chicken mixture, then cover with a sheet of greased foil and bake for 1½ to 2 hours, or until the timballo is firm. Remove from the oven and leave to rest for a few minutes, then invert onto a plate to serve.

NOTE: Ziti is a long, tubular dried pasta from the south of Italy, with quite a thick diameter. You will find it in good delicatessens.

BERNARD FILS
A NONTRON.

Portuguese spatchcock

Serves 4

1 red onion, chopped
6 garlic cloves, chopped
3 teaspoons grated lemon zest
2 teaspoons chilli flakes
1 1/2 teaspoons paprika
3 tablespoons olive oil
3 tablespoons red wine vinegar
4 x 500 g (1 lb 2 oz) spatchcocks (poussin)
lemon halves, to serve

Put the onion, garlic, lemon zest, chilli flakes, paprika, olive oil and vinegar in a food processor and blend until a smooth paste forms.

Using a large, sharp knife or kitchen scissors, cut through each spatchcock down either side of the backbone and discard the backbones. Turn the spatchcocks breast side up. Using the heel of your hand, press down firmly on the breastbone to flatten the birds out.

Score the breasts and legs several times, cutting through the skin into the flesh, then brush the birds all over with the spice mixture. Place in a non-metallic dish and drizzle with any remaining spice mixture. Cover and refrigerate overnight.

Preheat a chargrill pan or barbecue chargrill plate to medium–low. Grill the spatchcocks for 10 minutes on each side, or until the juices run clear when pierced through the thigh. Meanwhile, grill the lemon halves for 5–6 minutes, or until nicely caramelised. Serve the spatchcocks with the grilled lemon halves.

Moroccan chicken stew

Serves 4

2 generous pinches of saffron threads
875 ml (30 fl oz/3 1/2 cups) chicken stock
1.5 kg (3 lb 5 oz) whole chicken, cut into 8 pieces (see the *coq au vin* recipe on page 200)
2–3 tablespoons olive oil
1 teaspoon coriander seeds
1 teaspoon cumin seeds
2 onions, chopped
4 garlic cloves, finely chopped
1/2 teaspoon ground ginger
1 tablespoon soft brown sugar
3/4 teaspoon harissa, or to taste (see Note)
1 cinnamon stick
200 ml (7 fl oz) dry white wine
400 g (14 oz) butternut pumpkin (squash), peeled and cut into cubes
75 g (2 1/2 oz/2/3 cup) pitted green olives
1 tablespoon finely chopped preserved lemon rind
1 tablespoon finely chopped coriander (cilantro)
1 tablespoon finely chopped mint

Put the saffron in a cup and mix in 2 tablespoons of the stock. Leave to soak for at least 1 hour.

Season the chicken pieces with sea salt and freshly ground black pepper. Heat 2 tablespoons of the olive oil in a large flameproof casserole dish or saucepan. Cook the chicken in batches over medium heat for 8–10 minutes, or until golden, turning often and adding another tablespoon of oil if necessary. Remove the chicken to a plate.

Meanwhile, put the coriander seeds in a small frying pan and dry-fry over medium–low heat for 2–3 minutes, or until fragrant. Tip into a mortar or an electric spice grinder. Dry-fry the cumin seeds for 2–3 minutes, then add to the coriander seeds and grind to a fine powder.

Discard all but 1 teaspoon of the oil from the casserole dish. Add the onion and sauté over medium heat for 5 minutes. Tip in the toasted spices and add the garlic, ginger and sugar. Cook, stirring, for a further 2 minutes.

Stir in the saffron mixture, harissa, cinnamon stick, remaining stock and wine. Add the chicken and bring the mixture to the boil. Reduce the heat, then cover and gently simmer for 20 minutes. Add the pumpkin and cover again. Simmer for a further 30 minutes, or until the chicken is cooked and the pumpkin is tender, turning the chicken once.

Using a slotted spoon, transfer the chicken, onion and pumpkin to a deep serving dish and keep warm. Bring the stock to the boil and cook until reduced by about two-thirds.

Stir in the olives and preserved lemon and cook for a few minutes to heat through. Season to taste with sea salt and freshly ground black pepper, adding a little more harissa if desired. Stir in the herbs, then pour the sauce over the chicken and serve.

NOTE: Harissa is a fiery chilli paste widely used in North African cooking. It is available from delicatessens or speciality food stores.

Slow-cooked salted duck breasts

Serves 4

- 4 cloves
- 2 anise seeds (see Note)
- 2 teaspoons cracked black pepper
- 4 bay leaves
- 2 garlic cloves, chopped
- 115 g (4 oz/½ cup) coarse butcher's salt (available from good butchers)
- 4 duck breasts
- 3 tablespoons pomegranate molasses
- 2 teaspoons olive oil

Preheat the oven to 180°C (350°F/Gas 4). Using a mortar and pestle or an electric spice grinder, coarsely grind the cloves, anise seeds, pepper and bay leaves until a fine powder forms. Tip into a small roasting tin, stir in the garlic and butcher's salt and bake for 7–10 minutes, or until fragrant.

Dry the duck breasts with paper towels or a clean tea towel (dish towel), then trim off any excess fat. Lightly sprinkle with 3 tablespoons of the spice mixture — reserve the remaining mixture for another use. Place the duck in a single layer in a ceramic or glass dish, then cover with plastic wrap and refrigerate for 18–24 hours.

Rinse the duck breasts well and pat dry. Bring a large saucepan of water to the boil. Add one duck breast, boil for 1 minute, then remove. Repeat with the remaining breasts. Thoroughly pat them dry and leave to cool.

Brush the cooled breasts with the pomegranate molasses, coating evenly. Set aside to dry. Lay the breasts in a single layer in a ceramic or glass dish, then refrigerate, uncovered, to dry overnight.

Remove the duck from the refrigerator 30 minutes before cooking. Preheat the oven to 120°C (235°F/Gas ½).

Heat the olive oil in a large frying pan. Add two of the duck breasts, skin side down, and cook over medium–high heat for 4–5 minutes, or until deep brown underneath, then place skin side up in a large roasting tin, leaving space between each breast. Repeat with the remaining breasts.

Transfer to the oven and bake for 1 hour. Remove from the oven, cover loosely with foil and leave to rest in a warm place for 10 minutes. Carve into thin slices and serve.

NOTE: Anise seed, also sometimes called anise, is a sweet, aromatic spice widely used in confectionery, medicines and as a flavouring in alcohol (notably the French *pastis* and Greek *ouzo*). It is native to the Mediterranean region and south-west Asia and can be found in speciality food stores.

Spanish duck with smoked paprika, pears and toasted almonds

Serves 4

FOR THE STOCK
1 tablespoon olive oil
1 small carrot, cut into chunks
1 onion, cut into chunks
2 bay leaves
1 thyme sprig
1 parsley sprig
6 black peppercorns

2 kg (4 lb 8 oz) whole duck, cut into 8 pieces (you can follow the same jointing instructions outlined in the *coq au vin* recipe on page 200)
1/4 teaspoon freshly ground nutmeg
1/2 teaspoon sweet smoked paprika
a pinch of ground cloves
1 tablespoon olive oil
8 shallots, peeled
8 baby carrots, trimmed
2 garlic cloves, cut into slivers
4 tablespoons rich cream sherry
1 cinnamon stick
4 firm ripe pears, cut in half and cored
60 g (2 1/4 oz/heaped 1/3 cup) whole blanched almonds, roasted
2 1/2 tablespoons grated dark bittersweet chocolate

Make the stock a day ahead using the wings and neck of the duck. Heat the olive oil in a large saucepan, add the duck wings, neck, carrot and onion and cook over medium heat, stirring occasionally, for 15–20 minutes, or until browned. Add 1.25 litres (44 fl oz/5 cups) cold water, the bay leaves, thyme and parsley sprigs and peppercorns. Bring to the boil, then reduce the heat to low. Cover and simmer for 2 hours. Strain the stock, discarding the solids, then set aside to cool. Refrigerate overnight. The next day, remove the fat.

Preheat the oven to 180°C (350°F/Gas 4).

In a small bowl, combine the nutmeg, paprika and cloves with a little sea salt and freshly ground black pepper. Dust the duck pieces with the spice mixture. Heat the olive oil in a flameproof casserole dish, then brown the duck pieces in batches for 6–7 minutes over medium–high heat, turning once. Set the duck aside.

Drain off all but 1 teaspoon of fat from the casserole dish. Add the shallots and carrots and sauté over medium heat for 3–4 minutes, or until lightly browned. Add the garlic and cook for a further 2 minutes. Add the sherry and stir well to loosen any bits stuck to the bottom of the pan, then add the duck stock, cinnamon stick and all the duck pieces.

Bring to the boil, then cover with a tight-fitting lid and transfer to the oven. Bake for 1 hour 10 minutes, turning the duck halfway through. Add the pears and bake for a further 20 minutes, or until the duck is tender.

Meanwhile, process the almonds in a food processor until finely ground. Tip into a bowl, add the chocolate and stir to combine.

Using a slotted spoon, remove the duck and pears from the stock and transfer to a serving dish with the carrots, shallots and cinnamon stick. Cover and keep warm.

Bring the stock to the boil, then cook over high heat for 7–10 minutes, or until reduced by half. Add 3 tablespoons of the hot liquid to the almond and chocolate mixture, stir well, then whisk into the reduced sauce to thicken. Season to taste, pour over the duck and serve.

Chicken with lemon, parsley, pecorino and orecchiette

Serves 4

- 375 g (13 oz) dried orecchiette or other pasta shapes
- 2 tablespoons extra virgin olive oil
- 60 g (2 1/4 oz) butter
- 4 small boneless, skinless chicken breasts
- 4 tablespoons lemon juice
- 2 large handfuls of finely chopped flat-leaf (Italian) parsley
- 3 tablespoons toasted pine nuts
- 90 g (3 1/4 oz/1 cup) grated pecorino cheese
- lemon wedges, to serve

Cook the pasta in a saucepan of boiling salted water until *al dente*. Drain and return to the pan to keep warm.

Meanwhile, heat the olive oil and half the butter in a large heavy-based frying pan. Add the chicken breasts and cook over medium heat for 2 minutes on each side, then remove from the pan — the chicken will not be quite cooked through.

Add the lemon juice, parsley, pine nuts and remaining butter to the pan. Cook, stirring, for 1–2 minutes, or until the butter has melted and the mixture is well combined. Return the chicken breasts to the pan and cook over low heat for 3–4 minutes, or until the chicken is cooked through, turning once. Season with sea salt and freshly ground black pepper.

Pour the pan juices over the pasta. Add the pecorino to the pasta, toss well, then divide among four warmed bowls. Top each bowl with a chicken breast and serve immediately with lemon wedges.

Duck a l'orange

Serves 4

5 oranges
2 kg (4 lb 8 oz) whole duck
2 cinnamon sticks
a large handful of mint
95 g (3¼ oz/½ cup) soft brown sugar
125 ml (4 fl oz/½ cup) cider vinegar
4 tablespoons Grand Marnier or other orange-flavoured liqueur
30 g (1 oz) butter

Preheat the oven to 150°C (300°F/Gas 2). Cut two oranges in half and rub them all over the duck. Place the orange halves inside the duck cavity with the cinnamon sticks and mint. Tie the duck legs together with kitchen string, then tuck the wings under the birds and tie them in place. Prick the skin all over with a carving fork.

Put the duck on a rack, breast side down, inside a shallow roasting tin. Roast for 45 minutes, turning it over halfway through.

Meanwhile, remove the rind from the remaining oranges. Squeeze the juice from the oranges and set aside. Using a small, sharp knife, remove all the white pith from the rind, then very finely cut the rind.

Add the orange rind to a small saucepan of boiling water and boil for 1 minute. Drain, rinse well and drain again. Repeat this process twice using fresh boiling water each time. Set aside.

Heat the sugar in a saucepan over low heat until it melts and caramelises, swirling the pan gently so it caramelises evenly. When the sugar is a rich brown, add the vinegar and boil for 3 minutes, then add the reserved orange juice and Grand Marnier and simmer for 2 minutes.

Pour the excess fat from the roasting tin. Increase the oven temperature to 180°C (350°F/Gas 4). Spoon some of the orange sauce over the duck. Roast for 45 minutes, spooning the remaining sauce over the duck every 10 minutes and turning the duck to baste all sides.

Remove the duck from the oven, cover loosely with foil and leave to rest in a warm place for 10 minutes.

Meanwhile, strain the pan juices back into a saucepan, skim off any excess fat, then add the reserved orange rind and butter. Bring to a simmer, stirring to melt the butter, then serve with the duck.

Roast turkey breast with parsley crust

Serves 8

60 g (2 1/4 oz) butter
4 spring onions (scallions), finely chopped
2 garlic cloves, crushed
160 g (5 1/2 oz/2 cups) fresh white breadcrumbs
2 tablespoons chopped flat-leaf (Italian) parsley
1 kg (2 lb 4 oz) turkey breast
1 egg, lightly beaten

RASPBERRY AND REDCURRANT SAUCE
150 g (5 1/2 oz/1 1/4 cups) fresh or frozen raspberries
3 tablespoons orange juice
160 g (5 1/2 oz/1/2 cup) cranberry sauce
2 teaspoons dijon mustard
1 teaspoon finely grated orange zest
3 tablespoons port

Preheat the oven to 180°C (350°F/Gas 4). Melt the butter in a frying pan over medium heat. Add the spring onion and garlic and stir for several minutes, or until softened. Stir in the breadcrumbs and parsley, then remove from the heat and set aside to cool.

Place the turkey breast in a deep baking dish, skin side up, and brush with the beaten egg. Press the breadcrumb mixture onto the turkey in an even layer. Bake for 45 minutes, or until the crust is golden. Remove from the oven, cover loosely with foil and leave to rest in a warm place for 15–20 minutes.

Meanwhile, make the raspberry and redcurrant sauce. Press the raspberries through a sieve into a saucepan, discarding the seeds. Add the orange juice, cranberry sauce, mustard and orange zest and stir until smooth. Stir in the port, then simmer for 5 minutes. Remove from the heat and allow to cool.

Slice the turkey breast and serve drizzled with the sauce.

Duck breasts with walnut and pomegranate sauce

Serves 4

4 large duck breasts
1 onion, finely chopped
250 ml (9 fl oz/1 cup) fresh pomegranate juice (see Note)
2 tablespoons lemon juice
2 tablespoons soft brown sugar
1 teaspoon ground cinnamon
185 g (6½ oz/1½ cups) chopped walnuts
pomegranate seeds, to garnish (optional)

Preheat the oven to 180°C (350°F/Gas 4). Using a large, sharp knife, score each duck breast two or three times through the skin, taking care not to cut into the flesh.

Place a non-stick frying pan over high heat. Add two of the duck breasts, skin side down, and cook for 6 minutes, or until the skin is crisp and most of the fat has rendered out. Remove from the pan and repeat with the remaining breasts. Place in a single layer in a baking dish, skin side up.

Drain all but 1 tablespoon of fat from the pan. Add the onion and sauté over medium–high heat for 5–6 minutes, or until golden. Add the pomegranate juice, lemon juice, sugar, cinnamon and 125 g (4½ oz/1 cup) of the walnuts. Cook for 1 minute, then pour the mixture over the duck breasts. Transfer to the oven and bake for 15 minutes.

Remove the duck to a warmed plate, cover loosely with foil and leave to rest in a warm place for 5 minutes.

Skim any excess fat from the sauce. Carve the duck breasts and spoon the sauce over. Garnish with the remaining walnuts and the pomegranate seeds, if using.

NOTE: If fresh pomegranate juice isn't available, use 3 tablespoons pomegranate molasses, mixed with 185 ml (6 fl oz/¾ cup) water.

Duck confit

Serves 6

SPICE MIX

- 3 juniper berries, crushed
- 2 bay leaves, crushed
- 2 garlic cloves, crushed
- 2 tablespoons chopped rosemary
- 3 tablespoons thyme
- 1/4 teaspoon powdered mace or ground nutmeg
- 1 tablespoon sea salt
- 1 tablespoon freshly ground black pepper

- 12 duck leg quarters
- 2 kg (4 lb 8 oz) duck or goose fat (see Note)
- 4 garlic cloves, crushed
- 2 tablespoons thyme

In a bowl, mix together all the spice mix ingredients. Liberally sprinkle the spice mix all over the duck legs, rubbing it in well, then place them in a non-metallic container. Cover and refrigerate for 12–48 hours.

Rinse the duck legs and pat dry with paper towels. Melt the duck fat in a large, deep saucepan over low heat, then add the garlic, thyme and duck legs. Cook over very low heat for 2 1/2–3 hours, or until the meat is very soft — do not allow the fat to simmer vigorously (the surface should barely tremble) or the duck will become stringy.

Transfer the duck legs to a deep ceramic, glass or non-reactive metal container and set aside to cool. When the fat has cooled a little, strain it and pour over the duck legs, making sure they are completely covered with the fat. Cover and refrigerate. Confit will keep, refrigerated, for 2–3 months.

To serve, lift the duck pieces out of the fat, place in a baking dish and roast them in a 180°C (350°F/Gas 4) oven for 15–20 minutes. Serve warm.

NOTE: You can save the fat rendered from the other duck recipes in this chapter to use in duck confit or for roasting potatoes — strain it thoroughly and refrigerate for several months. You can also buy duck or goose fat from good delicatessens and gourmet food stores.

Turkey roll with blood orange sauce

Serves 8

90 g ($3\frac{1}{4}$ oz/$\frac{1}{2}$ cup) dried apricots, chopped
30 g (1 oz) butter
1 onion, finely chopped
1 garlic clove, crushed
400 g (14 oz) minced (ground) chicken
120 g ($4\frac{1}{4}$ oz/$1\frac{1}{2}$ cups) fresh breadcrumbs
75 g ($2\frac{1}{2}$ oz/$\frac{1}{2}$ cup) currants
70 g ($2\frac{1}{2}$ oz/$\frac{1}{2}$ cup) pistachio nuts, toasted and chopped
3 tablespoons chopped flat-leaf (Italian) parsley
3.4 kg (7 lb 13 oz) whole boned turkey (ask your butcher to do this for you)
oil, for brushing

BLOOD ORANGE SAUCE
2 blood oranges
2 tablespoons sugar
1 tablespoon brandy
250 ml (9 fl oz/1 cup) blood orange juice
4 tablespoons chicken stock
3 teaspoons cornflour (cornstarch)

Put the apricots in a small bowl, cover with boiling water and soak for 30 minutes. Preheat the oven to 180°C (350°F/Gas 4).

Melt the butter in a frying pan. Add the onion and garlic and sauté over medium heat for 5 minutes, or until softened. Transfer to a bowl and add the well-drained apricots, the chicken, breadcrumbs, currants, nuts and parsley. Season with sea salt and freshly ground black pepper and mix well.

Place the turkey on a work surface, skin side down, then place the stuffing mixture down the length of the turkey, in a neat sausage shape. Fold the turkey over to enclose the stuffing, then secure with toothpicks. Using kitchen string, tie the roll at 3 cm ($1\frac{1}{4}$ inch) intervals to form a neat shape.

Place the turkey on a lightly greased baking tray. (If your turkey is too large for your baking tray, cut the turkey in half — this will also make it easier to roll.) Rub with a little oil and season. Roast for $1\frac{1}{2}$–2 hours, or until the juices run clear. Remove from the oven, cover loosely with foil and leave to rest in a warm place for 10–15 minutes.

Meanwhile, make the blood orange sauce. Using a small, sharp knife, remove the skin from the oranges in neat strips. Reserve one-third and discard the rest. Remove as much white pith as possible from the reserved strips, then cut into very fine slices. Remove all the white pith from the oranges. Cut between the membranes to remove the segments, catching any juices over a bowl as you do so. Set aside.

Place the rind strips in a saucepan, cover with cold water and bring to the boil. Drain well, then repeat. Set aside.

Sprinkle the sugar over the base of a saucepan over medium heat and stir until the sugar has dissolved and is a light caramel colour. Remove from the heat, cool, then stir in the brandy. Return to the heat, stir to dissolve any solid caramel, then add the orange juice (including any reserved juices) and stock and bring to a simmer. Mix the cornflour with 1 tablespoon of water, add to the sauce and stir over medium heat until it boils and thickens. Add the orange segments and rind strips, stirring until heated through. Season to taste.

Carefully remove the string and toothpicks from the warm turkey roll. Cut into slices and serve with the sauce.

Roast turkey with chestnut and prosciutto stuffing

Serves 8

STUFFING
100 g (3½ oz) prosciutto, finely chopped
220 g (7¾ oz) minced (ground) pork
220 g (7¾ oz) minced (ground) chicken
1 egg
90 ml (3 fl oz) thick (double/heavy) cream
175 g (6 oz/⅓ cup) chestnut purée
½ teaspoon finely chopped fresh sage, or ¼ teaspoon dried sage
a pinch of cayenne pepper

3 kg (6 lb 12 oz) turkey
300 g (10½ oz) butter, softened
1 onion, roughly chopped
4 sage leaves
1 rosemary sprig
½ celery stalk, cut into 2–3 pieces
1 carrot, cut into 3–4 pieces
250 ml (9 fl oz/1 cup) dry white wine
125 ml (4 fl oz/½ cup) dry marsala
250 ml (9 fl oz/1 cup) chicken stock
mustard fruits, to serve

Preheat the oven to 170°C (325°F/Gas 3). Combine all the stuffing ingredients in a bowl, season well with sea salt and freshly ground black pepper and mix thoroughly.

Fill the turkey cavity with the stuffing and sew up the opening with kitchen string. Cross the legs and tie them together, then tuck the wings behind the body. Rub the skin with 100 g (3½ oz) of the butter. Put the chopped onion in the centre of a large roasting tin and place the turkey on top, breast side up. Add another 100 g (3½ oz) of butter to the tin with the sage, rosemary, celery and carrot, then pour the wine and marsala over.

Roast for 2½–3 hours, basting several times with the pan juices and covering the turkey breast with buttered baking paper when the skin becomes golden brown. Transfer the turkey to a large warmed plate, cover loosely with foil and leave to rest in a warm place for 30 minutes.

Transfer the vegetables from the pan to a food processor and blend to a smooth purée. Add the pan juices and any scrapings from the base of the tin and process until well blended. Transfer to a saucepan, add the remaining butter and stock and bring to the boil. Season and cook until thickened to a thick pouring consistency, then transfer to a gravy boat.

Carve the turkey and serve with the stuffing, gravy and mustard fruits.

game

Long throughout history, wild beasts and fowl were an essential part of the human food chain and... well, fair game. Before animals and birds were domesticated, they had to be hunted if they were wanted for food. Over more recent centuries, hunting for game has come to be associated with sporting pleasures and with the wealthy, who controlled the land the animals roamed on.

These days the word 'game' connotes creatures that are shot for sport, although many species that were traditionally only available from the wild are now farmed on a commercial scale and are still called 'game'.

There are two main varieties of game: furred and feathered. In North America, bear and bison, caribou and muskrat, elk, racoon and squirrel are all considered game, while in Africa, antelope, ostrich and zebra are in the shooters' sights. In Australia one can dine on emu, kangaroo and crocodile, and in the United Kingdom snipe, woodcock, grouse and partridge. In Italy, Hungary and other European nations, people keenly hunt the flavoursome *cinghiale* or wild boar; in Spain, a species of ibex is among the favoured quarry.

In most countries, game is given legal protections under acts of parliament and international wildlife legislation, although some nations have more liberal laws than others. In continental Europe, for example, there is a tradition of hunting and eating small songbirds such as larks, thrush and the unfortunate ortalan, whereas the English have long outlawed such practices. Consuming ortalan is now banned, which apparently didn't stop François

Mitterand from famously dining on a few at his final meal in 1996. These tiny birds — weighing only 25 g (barely an ounce) — were captured live, kept in darkness and fattened by force feeding until four times their weight. 'True' gourmands then killed them by drowning them in Armagnac, and the birds were cooked and eaten whole — guts, bones, beak and all. The diner was supposed to eat these birds with a white napkin held over his face so he could savour the aromas and also 'hide from God', presumably out of guilt. It is rumoured that illegal ortalan eating still occurs in France.

Deer, rabbit, hare, pheasant, boar, quail, duck, pigeon and partridge are among the most likely wild game one may encounter; readily available farmed examples include rabbit, quail, pheasant, venison and guinea fowl. The characteristics of farmed game are very different to feral game, which have an enormously varied diet and lead a highly active, free-range existence. Wild game is very rich and deep in flavour, with lean, somewhat firm meat that requires special treatment to tenderise. It can vary markedly, according to the age, condition and diet of the animal. Many diners prefer the relative mildness and predictable qualities of farmed game, while others relish the assertive, savoury and unmistakeable taste of feral game. Both types are admirable in their own way — and were it not for farmed birds and deer, many of us would probably never get to taste game at all.

Hanging game

Some hunters don't hang their kill at all, enjoying it when it is chewy and quite mild tasting; at the other extreme, some serious gourmands like their game so well-hung that it smells and tastes rank. The fashion these days falls somewhere between the two.

Hanging wild game develops tenderness and flavour. This process must be carried out in a well-ventilated, cool and dry environment to discourage the growth of harmful bacteria. While the game hangs, enzymes work on the flesh, tenderising it and releasing those 'gamey' flavours so associated with wild meat. The longer it hangs, the stronger its flavours, and the warmer the conditions, the more quickly it takes these on.

Birds are hung unplucked and undrawn (with their entrails intact) for one to seven days, depending on their size. They must be hung singly as contact with other hanging game causes the flesh to rot. Small furred beasts such as rabbits and hare are hung unskinned and ungutted for just a day, while deer needs to be gutted and bled first, then hung for about a week, although some prefer venison after two or even three weeks of hanging.

Farmed quail and farmed rabbit gain nothing from hanging and are cooked fresh.

GAME BIRDS

The majority of game birds most readily available from supermarkets and butchers are subject to intensive farming practices every bit as awful as those suffered by other poultry. There are very few free-range — let alone organic — suppliers of game, although more producers are striving to make concessions towards more 'natural' and humane rearing practices.

Because of the innate habits of many of these birds (roosting, hiding among grasses, living in coveys, migrating long distances), many are difficult to farm according to true free-range practices, but do try to find game birds that are at least 'range' reared if free-range or organic options are not available. In 'range' rearing, the birds are still enclosed, but in roomy pens with plenty of room to roam, fly, dust-bathe and feed at will.

Look for ones with unblemished skin, with no tears or signs of other damage, and make sure they have been thoroughly plucked. Where possible, buy birds with necks, feet and even heads still attached as these can be used to make flavoursome stocks or sauces.

PHEASANT

There are 49 species and numerous sub-species of pheasant. The bird we best know as a 'pheasant', the ring-necked pheasant, is one of the world's most beautiful birds. The rooster in particular has glorious plumage, with a green and red head, patterned, bronze body feathers and the characteristic white ringed detail around its neck. Its long, striped tail feathers are another distinguishing characteristic, as is its distinct call.

Alexander the Great reputedly introduced pheasants into Greece some 2500 years ago. Pheasants were frequently served at ancient Roman banquets. The Romans farmed pheasants, fattening them on a special mixture made from locusts, ant eggs, olive oil and flour. They were also an important component of the Romans' living larder, a collection of live beasts they took with them to their far-flung colonies, including England. Small numbers of pheasants were imported into the United States from 1733, but it wasn't until 100 pairs of Chinese ring-necked pheasants were released in Oregon in 1881 that the bird really became established there.

Pheasants live on the ground, under forest or scrub cover and feed off the ground on leaves, insects, seeds and grains. They can fly, but in short bursts. The rooster pheasant grows up to 90 cm (36 inches) in length, although half of this length is tail, and weighs up to 1.8 kg (4 lb). The less spectacular-looking hen pheasant weighs up to 1.1 kg (2½ lb).

Pheasant flesh is tough if not hung for a period of time. It is most commonly roasted, although it can also be pot-roasted whole, or cut into pieces and braised. Like all game, pheasant is extremely lean, so care must be taken that the flesh doesn't dry out — place slices of thinly sliced pork back fat, pancetta or bacon over the breast when roasting.

These lean birds are not suitable for grilling or barbecuing, although the breasts can be sautéed over medium heat in a little oil or butter.

Like most feathered game, pheasant teams well with deeply savoury flavours — sage, juniper berries, rosemary, bacon, lentils, garlic, sauerkraut, sausage, dried and fresh mushrooms, full-bodied red wine — as well as sweet ones in the form of prunes, plums, honey, citrus, madeira and sherry, caramelised onions, figs and apples.

Quail

Quails are distributed widely around the world. The North American quails are a different species to those found in Europe, Asia and Africa; the latter are part of the pheasant family. The North American quails are also found in Australasia, British Colombia and Chile. Quails, of which there are many varieties, are small, round birds that inhabit covered grassy, tussocky terrain. They are relatively easy prey as they prefer running to flying, but nowadays most cooks enjoy the convenience of farmed quail.

Farmed quails are tender, lean and a little 'gamey' tasting, but they in no way resemble their assertively flavoured and quite tough-textured wild cousins. The recipes in this chapter are suited to farmed quail. These versatile little birds can be grilled, roasted, fried or braised. They typically weigh about 200 g (7 oz) each — allow one per person as an entrée, or two per person if serving as a main course (they are usually sold in trays of six).

Quail should never be overcooked — leave it a little pink in the middle or it will be hard and tasteless. Whole quail will roast in a 180–200°C (350–400°F/Gas 4–6) oven in 15 minutes, and will cook on a medium–hot barbecue or chargrill pan in just 6–7 minutes. To grill quail, it first needs to be 'butterflied' so it will cook evenly. To do this, remove the backbone, place the bird breast side up on a chopping board, then use the heel of your hand to break the breastbone, striking the breast firmly several times to flatten the bird out.

Quail can also be cut into quarters (giving two breasts and two whole legs) and sautéed; just 3 minutes of cooking per side, in a heavy-based pan with a little olive oil or a mixture of oil and butter, is all it needs.

Quail pairs beautifully with many strong flavours and is especially memorable with rosemary, bacon, sage, balsamic vinegar, raisins, chestnuts, caramelised onions, lentils, mushrooms, honey, prunes, juniper berries and sweet, fruit-based jellies, relishes and chutneys.

Pigeon and squab

Wood pigeons, related to doves, occur throughout North America and Europe, extending as far east as India. Because these migratory birds are so plentiful they are an agricultural nuisance in many parts of the world, notably Europe, and are frequently hunted to control numbers. Cooks who don't have access to wild-shot pigeons must 'make do' with farmed equivalents, which more often than not are sold as 'squab'.

Squab are pigeons that are killed at about four weeks of age, before they have ever flown. Some of the most popular varieties include the Red Carneau and the White King. The Egyptian pharaohs apparently loved squab, and it's not hard to see why. Their flavour is a little gamey, but not overly so, and they have a small amount of fat — an unusual quality for game meat. Because their muscles have never really worked, the meat is utterly tender. Each bird weighs a relatively meaty 300–500 g (10½ oz–1 lb 2 oz) when dressed, a generous serving for one person.

Never cook these tender birds beyond medium–rare. They are best suited to roasting (either whole or jointed), pan-frying (in pieces), or grilling (in pieces or butterflied — see instructions opposite for butterflying quail).

Guinea fowl

The guinea fowl is native to sub-Saharan Africa. The ancient Egyptians knew this bird well; it is believed they (and the Greeks) bred them in incubators, for the table. The Romans regarded both their meat and eggs as great delicacies. Portuguese traders, who called the bird 'pintada' or 'painted hen', brought the bird home from the colony of Guinea around the fifteenth century and it quickly became popular throughout Europe. The guinea fowl also ended up, thanks to Spanish slave trading vessels, in the Caribbean.

A large, hardy bird, the guinea fowl is a prodigious eater of insects such as mosquitoes, ticks, fleas and other pests, making it a popular farmyard bird. It also has a loud, distinctive cry when disturbed and many farmers value it as a 'watchdog'. Guinea fowl are very sociable and live in small, tight-knit groups. They mate for life and weigh up to 1.8 kg (4 lb) when fully grown.

Their meat is only slightly gamey and is extremely lean. Unlike pheasant and some other game birds, they don't have any tough leg or thigh tendons, and their meat is relatively tender. Their milder flavour and hefty size makes them a worthy substitute for chicken in most chicken recipes.

They can be roasted whole, but do cover the breast with bacon slices to keep it moist, and also baste regularly. Guinea fowl are perfect for pot-roasting whole or braising in pieces; they can also be poached or pan-fried. They should be cooked all the way through, just until their juices run clear.

Like other game birds, their flavour complements those of fruits (plums, citrus, apple), chestnuts, herbs (sage, thyme, rosemary), honey, salty pork meats such as pancetta, bacon and prosciutto, as well as cider, wine, balsamic vinegar, truffles, foie gras, lentils and garlic.

FURRED GAME

Venison

'Venison' is a word for deer meat that also includes elk, moose and caribou. Archaeological evidence suggests deer was eaten even before cows, pigs or sheep. Worldwide there are around 35 types and their distribution is far flung.

Today, more venison is consumed than all the other game meats combined. The meat is a deep blood-red and is extremely lean and low in cholesterol. Farming maintains good supply and the animals are reared in a largely natural, unforced way — deer are ruminants and farming practices allow them to essentially graze on pasture and grow at their own rate. The slaughter age varies from 12 to 30 months.

Farmed venison is slightly less lean and deeply flavoured than its wild counterpart, but is also more tender as the animals are not as active. Whether farmed or wild, venison must be hung to tenderise the flesh and allow flavour to develop — this aging period should be about two weeks if the animal has a good covering of fat on it.

The primary cuts are the leg (or haunch), the saddle (taken from the upper middle section and including the eye fillet), the breast (sometimes called the flank) and the shoulder (including the neck).

The leg and saddle are prime roasting cuts; the saddle can also be cut into cutlets, which are superb when grilled or sautéed. The eye fillet is perfect for roasting whole or, when cut into steaks, grilling, sautéing or barbecuing.

The shoulder, neck and flank are tough cuts and are best braised into a hearty stew, or minced (ground) and used in burgers, sauces, pie fillings or sausages. Braised venison shanks make excellent eating and, when sliced through the bone crossways, make a fabulous osso bucco.

When cooking large pieces of venison, take care they don't dry out and toughen. For this reason, they were traditionally 'larded' — strips of pork fat were threaded into a larding needle and inserted into the meat (this can also be done by piercing the meat all over with a sharp knife and pushing fat into the incisions). The melting fat kept the meat lubricated during cooking. Adding fat to meat is now out of fashion, but on the flipside, we now enjoy rarer meat than in days gone by. To stop prime cuts of venison drying out, cook them to no more than medium–rare when roasting, grilling or frying

— or rare if you enjoy meat cooked that way. Of course you can still lard very lean meats such as venison, either with pork fat, fatty bacon, or perhaps a paste made from finely chopped pancetta and rosemary, seasoned well with freshly ground black pepper.

Venison tastes great with all the strong-flavoured ingredients that so complement other game: port, red wine, brandy, cider, ale and Armagnac are good alcohols to include in a sauce or braising liquid. It is good with sweet and acidic fruits such as dark berries, currants, sour cherries, prunes, raisins, orange and plums, and excellent with chestnuts, bacon, pancetta, fresh and dried mushrooms, sage, rosemary, thyme, lentils, walnuts, olives, anchovies, beetroot, horseradish and warm spices.

Rabbit

This cute, canny, furry animal is variously considered a pet, a pest and a useful source of food. Prodigious breeders, they are considered a scourge in some countries to which they were introduced (such as New Zealand and Australia), chewing and burrowing their way through crops, forests and pasture land.

The European rabbit, often called the 'true' rabbit, is native to Iberia. Today, only Antarctica is free of wild rabbits. The American cottontail rabbit, of which there are many types, is a different species to the European rabbit, from which more than 80 varieties of domesticated rabbit have been bred.

Farmed rabbits are killed at about 12 weeks and are often raised under the same woeful, intensive conditions as their chicken friends, so exercise care when buying farmed rabbit. Many butchers and specialist game meat suppliers can obtain wild rabbit.

Farmed rabbit is milder and paler than wild rabbit; it is also moister and somewhat sweet. The wild meat is browny pink, while farmed meat is nearly white. Some people describe the taste of farmed rabbit as similar to chicken as it is only mildly gamey. But really, its flavour is quite its own.

Rabbit meat is very lean. Older animals are best braised as they will otherwise be tough and dry. Younger specimens, and certainly farmed rabbit, can be roasted or pot-roasted whole.

It is also possible that you'll be able to buy various cuts of rabbit — the legs (both hind and fore) are excellent for braising, while the saddle (the top middle section) is best roasted.

Rabbit tastes glorious roasted with garlic, fennel seeds, rosemary and pancetta or prosciutto, which is how they like them in central Italy. To complement their delicate, sweet flavour, braise them with mild and slightly sweet flavours such as those of good stock, mushrooms, onions, mustard, cream, brandy, prunes, bacon, onions, lemon, garlic, chestnuts and pine nuts.

Rabbit and mushroom rillettes

Serves 8

1.3 kg (3 lb) rabbit
750 g (1 lb 10 oz) pork belly, bones and rind removed
500 g (1 lb 2 oz) pork belly fat
6 button mushrooms, finely sliced
10 g (¼ oz) dried porcini mushrooms
½ teaspoon ground nutmeg
½ teaspoon ground cloves
½ teaspoon ground cinnamon
1 garlic clove, crushed
125 ml (4 fl oz/½ cup) white wine
thyme, to garnish
thin slices of toast, to serve

Preheat the oven to 120°C (235°F/Gas ½). Wash the rabbit, pat dry with paper towels, then cut into four even-sized pieces. Cut the pork belly into large chunks and the pork belly fat into small cubes. Put all the meat, pork fat and button mushrooms in a 3 litre (105 fl oz/12 cup) casserole dish.

Put the porcini mushrooms in a small bowl, cover with 125 ml (4 fl oz/½ cup) hot water and leave to soak for 5 minutes. Drain the porcini, reserving the liquid, then squeeze dry and roughly chop. Return the porcini mushrooms to the soaking liquid and add the ground spices, garlic and wine. Mix to combine, then pour over the meat mixture, using clean hands to thoroughly combine.

Cover with a tightly fitting lid and bake for 4 hours, or until the meat is very tender and falling off the bone. Season with sea salt and freshly ground black pepper. Set a large sieve over a bowl, then put the casserole contents into the sieve and leave to drain well. Reserve the strained juices, and allow the solids to cool.

When cool, remove and discard the bones from the rabbit. Use two forks to finely shred the rabbit and pork belly, discarding the fat from the pork belly. Divide the shredded meats among eight 125 ml (4 fl oz/½ cup) ramekins. Strain the reserved fat and juices through a fine seive, then pour over the meat to cover well.

Cover the ramekins and refrigerate overnight to allow the flavours to develop. Turn the rillettes out of the ramekins, garnish with thyme and serve with thin slices of toast.

Rabbit fricassee

Serves 4

1.5 kg (3 lb 5 oz) rabbit
60 g (2 1/4 oz) clarified butter
200 g (7 oz) button mushrooms
125 ml (4 fl oz/1/2 cup) white wine
125 ml (4 fl oz/1/2 cup) chicken stock
1 bouquet garni
4 tablespoons olive oil
20 g (3/4 oz/1 small bunch) sage, leaves picked
150 ml (5 fl oz) thick (double/heavy) cream
2 egg yolks

Using a large, sharp knife, cut through the hip bones of the rabbit on both sides to remove the hind legs. Cut through the collarbone and vertebrae to remove the front legs. Trim the carcass at either end and trim the flaps, discarding the off-cuts. Cut the saddle in half crossways, then cut the pieces in half again down the spine to give eight pieces in total.

Season the rabbit pieces with sea salt and freshly ground black pepper. Heat half the butter in a large saucepan. Fry in batches over medium–high heat for 6 minutes, turning to brown all over. Remove and set aside.

Melt the remaining butter in the pan, then add the mushrooms and sauté over medium heat for 5 minutes, or until browned. Return the rabbit to the pan, add the wine and boil for 2–3 minutes. Add the stock and bouquet garni, then cover and gently simmer over very low heat for 40 minutes.

Meanwhile, heat the olive oil in a small saucepan. Drop the sage leaves, a few at a time, into the hot oil; they will immediately start to bubble around the edges. Cook for 30 seconds, or until bright green and crisp, taking care not to overcook them or they will burn. Drain on paper towels and sprinkle with salt.

Using a slotted spoon, remove the rabbit and mushrooms from the simmering stock and keep warm. Discard the bouquet garni and remove the saucepan from the heat. In a bowl, mix together the cream and egg yolks, then stir quickly into the stock. Return over very low heat and cook, stirring constantly, for 5 minutes, or until thickened slightly — take care not to let the sauce boil or it will curdle. Season to taste.

Divide the rabbit and mushrooms among warmed serving plates. Drizzle with the sauce and garnish with the sage leaves.

Stuffed guinea fowl

Serves 4

- 100 g (3½ oz/½ cup) dried borlotti (cranberry) beans, soaked overnight, then drained
- 4 whole garlic cloves, peeled
- 1 bay leaf
- 4 tablespoons olive oil, plus extra, for brushing
- 25 g (1 oz) dried porcini mushrooms
- 75 g (3 oz/heaped ⅓ cup) green lentils
- 1 small onion, finely chopped
- 100 g (3½ oz) pancetta or smoked bacon, diced
- 1 sage sprig, chopped
- 100 g (3½ oz/⅔ cup) almonds or pistachios, lightly roasted, then chopped
- 1.5 kg (3 lb 5 oz) guinea fowl, boned, leaving the wings and lower legs intact (ask your butcher to do this)
- 2 tablespoons red wine

Put the beans in a saucepan, cover with water and bring to the boil, skimming off any scum that forms on the surface. Reduce the heat, add two of the garlic cloves, the bay leaf and 1 tablespoon of the olive oil. Simmer for 40–50 minutes, or until the beans are tender. Drain well.

Meanwhile, put the mushrooms in a bowl, add 150 ml (5 fl oz) hot water and leave to soak for 15 minutes. Cook the lentils in a saucepan of water with a garlic clove for 20 minutes, or until the lentils are soft but not mushy. Drain well, discarding the garlic clove.

Preheat the oven to 200°C (400°F/Gas 6). Heat the remaining olive oil in a frying pan. Add the onion and pancetta and sauté over medium heat for 5 minutes, or until the onion is soft and the pancetta lightly browned.

Drain the mushrooms, reserving the soaking liquid, then roughly chop. Finely chop the remaining garlic clove. Add the mushrooms and garlic to the frying pan with the sage, stirring to prevent browning. Add the drained beans, lentils and nuts, stirring well. Cook for a few minutes, then season to taste with sea salt and freshly ground black pepper.

Push the mixture into the bird cavity. Sew up the opening using thick cotton or thin string, or secure with toothpicks. (If you have any stuffing left over, bake it separately in a small covered greased dish for 20 minutes.) Tie the legs together and brush the bird with olive oil. Place in a baking dish and roast for 20 minutes, then reduce the oven temperature to 180°C (350°F/Gas 4) and cook for 20 minutes more.

Check the bird is cooked by piercing the thickest part of the thigh with a skewer; the juices should run clear. Check the stuffing is cooked by pushing a skewer into the cavity for 3 seconds: the skewer should feel very hot when you pull it out. If it isn't, cover the bird with foil and cook a little longer. Remove the bird from the oven, cover loosely with foil and leave to rest in a warm place for 15 minutes.

While the bird is resting, pour the pan juices into a small saucepan. Add the wine and reserved mushroom liquid and bring to the boil. Season to taste.

Carve the bird and serve drizzled with the sauce.

Barbecued quail

Serves 6

6 quails
250 ml (9 fl oz/1 cup) dry red wine
2 celery stalks, including the leafy tops, chopped
1 carrot, chopped
1 small onion, chopped
1 bay leaf, torn into small pieces
1 teaspoon allspice
1 teaspoon dried thyme
lemon wedges, to serve

GARLIC BASTE
2 garlic cloves, crushed
2 tablespoons olive oil
2 tablespoons lemon juice

Using poultry shears, cut down either side of the backbone of each quail, then discard the backbones. Place the birds on a work surface, breast side up. Open them out flat, then press firmly with the heel of your hand to flatten. Using a large sharp knife or poultry shears, cut each quail in half through the breast, then cut each piece in half again at the top of the leg to yield thigh and drumstick pieces, and breast and wing pieces.

In a non-metallic bowl, mix together the wine, celery, carrot, onion, bay leaf and allspice. Add the quail pieces and turn to coat, then cover and refrigerate for 3 hours, or preferably overnight, turning occasionally.

Drain the quail pieces and sprinkle with the thyme and plenty of sea salt and freshly ground black pepper. Whisk the garlic baste ingredients together in a small bowl.

Heat a lightly oiled barbecue flat plate, chargrill plate or chargrill pan to medium–high. Brushing occasionally with the garlic baste, cook the quail pieces, in batches if necessary, for 3–4 minutes on each side, or until cooked but slightly pink in the middle. Serve hot, with lemon wedges.

Quail wrapped in vine leaves with braised borlotti beans

Serves 4

BRAISED BORLOTTI BEANS
350 g (12 oz/1¾ cups) dried borlotti (cranberry) beans, soaked overnight, then drained
435 ml (15¼ fl oz/1¾ cups) dry red wine
1 small onion, finely chopped
3 cloves
3 tablespoons olive oil
1 tablespoon chopped rosemary
3 garlic cloves, crushed
a pinch of chilli flakes
3 tablespoons chopped parsley

4 rosemary sprigs
4 quails
2 tablespoons olive oil
1 tablespoon balsamic vinegar
2 teaspoons soft brown sugar
8 large vine leaves, preserved in brine

To braise the borlotti beans, put them in a large saucepan, add the wine, onion, cloves and 875 ml (30 fl oz/3½ cups) water. Bring to the boil, then reduce the heat and simmer for 25 minutes.

Meanwhile, heat the olive oil in a small saucepan. Add the rosemary, garlic and chilli flakes and stir over medium heat for 1–2 minutes, or until fragrant. Add the mixture to the beans and simmer for a further 45–60 minutes, or until the beans are tender.

Drain the beans, reserving the cooking liquid. Return the liquid to the saucepan and simmer until it has reduced and thickened. Add the beans, season with sea salt and freshly ground black pepper, then simmer for a further 5 minutes. Stir in the parsley, season to taste and allow to cool for 15 minutes before serving.

Meanwhile, preheat the oven to 180°C (350°F/Gas 4). Place a rosemary sprig in each quail cavity, then tie the legs together with kitchen string. Tuck the wings behind each bird.

Heat the olive oil in a large frying pan. Add the quails and cook over medium–high heat for 4–5 minutes, turning to brown all over. Add the vinegar and sugar to the pan, bring just to the boil, then remove from the heat.

Blanch the vine leaves in boiling water for 15 seconds. Drain well, then allow to cool. Wrap a vine leaf around each quail to enclose. Place them in a roasting tin, seam side down, and bake for 10–12 minutes, or until the quails are cooked but still a little pink. Serve with the braised borlotti beans.

Roast pheasant with pears

Serves 4–6

2 x 1 kg (2 lb 4 oz) pheasants
100 g (3½ oz) thin pancetta slices
8 thyme sprigs, plus 2 teaspoons thyme leaves
80 g (2¾ oz) butter, melted
3 corella pears, cut into quarters and cored
3 tablespoons apple cider
4 tablespoons pear liqueur
125 ml (4 fl oz/½ cup) pouring (whipping) cream

Preheat the oven to 230°C (450°C/Gas 8). Rinse the pheasants and pat dry with paper towels. Tuck the wings underneath the pheasants and tie the legs together with kitchen string. Wrap the pancetta slices around each pheasant, then tuck the thyme sprigs underneath the pancetta. Dip two large pieces of muslin (cheesecloth) into the melted butter and wrap one around each pheasant.

Place the pheasants on a rack in a flameproof baking dish. Roast for 10 minutes, then reduce the oven temperature to 200°C (400°C/Gas 6) and roast for 15 minutes. Add the pears to the dish and roast for a further 20 minutes, or until the juices of the pheasants run clear when the thighs are pierced with a skewer. Transfer the pheasants and pears to a warmed plate, discarding the muslin, then cover loosely with foil and leave to rest while making the sauce.

Place the baking dish with the juices on the stovetop. Add the cider and liqueur, bring to the boil and cook for 1 minute, or until reduced by half.

Strain into a clean saucepan, stir in the cream and boil for 5 minutes, or until the sauce thickens slightly. Stir in the thyme leaves and season well with sea salt and freshly ground black pepper. Serve with the pheasants and pears.

Quail with grapes and tarragon

Serves 4

8 quails
8 tarragon sprigs
2 tablespoons clarified butter
150 ml (5 fl oz) white wine
400 ml (14 fl oz) chicken stock
150 g (5½ oz) seedless green grapes

Season the quails well with sea salt and freshly ground black pepper and place a tarragon sprig in each.

Heat the butter in a large, deep frying pan. Add the quails and cook over medium–high heat for 6 minutes, turning to brown all over. Add the wine and boil for 30 seconds, then add the stock and grapes.

Cover the pan and simmer for 6–8 minutes, or until the quails are cooked through. Using a slotted spoon, remove the quails and grapes and keep warm. Boil the sauce until it has reduced by two-thirds and is syrupy, then strain and serve drizzled over the quails and grapes.

VENISON WITH BLACKBERRY SAUCE

SERVES 4

60 g (2¼ oz) clarified butter
12 baby onions
16 venison medallions, about 50 g (1¾ oz) each, cut from the eye fillet

BLACKBERRY SAUCE
150 g (5½ oz/1¼ cups) fresh or frozen blackberries or blackcurrants
3 tablespoons redcurrant jelly
3 tablespoons red wine
420 ml (14½ fl oz/1⅔ cups) beef or veal stock
10 g (¼ oz) butter, softened
½ tablespoon plain (all-purpose) flour

Melt half the butter in a saucepan, then add the onions. Cover and cook over low heat, stirring occasionally, for 20–25 minutes, or until the onions are golden and tender.

Meanwhile, start making the blackberry sauce. Put the berries and redcurrant jelly in a saucepan with 3 tablespoons water. Mix gently, then boil for 5 minutes, or until the fruit has softened and the liquid is syrupy. Set aside.

Season the venison with sea salt and freshly ground black pepper. Heat the remaining butter in a frying pan, then add the venison in batches and cook over high heat for 1–2 minutes, turning once. Remove and keep warm.

Add the wine to the pan and boil for 30 seconds, then add the stock and boil until reduced by half. Mix together the softened butter and flour to make a smooth paste, then whisk it into the stock. Stirring constantly, bring the mixture to the boil and cook for 2 minutes.

Strain the syrup from the berry mixture into the pan and stir together well. Season to taste with sea salt and freshly ground black pepper. Spoon the sauce over the venison and onions, using the drained fruit to garnish if desired.

Squab escabeche with sherry, saffron and orange

Serves 4–6

4 squabs, about 300 g (10½ oz) each
125 ml (4 fl oz/½ cup) olive oil
2 red onions, cut into rings
2 carrots, thinly sliced
1½ teaspoons smoked Spanish paprika
a large pinch of saffron threads
2 bay leaves
8 thyme sprigs
4 orange peel strips
500 ml (17 fl oz/2 cups) medium-dry sherry
125 ml (4 fl oz/½ cup) orange juice
125 ml (4 fl oz/½ cup) sherry vinegar

Preheat the oven to 180°C (350°F/Gas 4). Using a large, sharp knife, cut down along either side of the backbone on each squab and discard the backbone. Turn the birds breast side down on the cutting board and cut in half down the breastbone to give two pieces, then cut off the legs through the hip joint to give four pieces.

Heat 2 tablespoons of the olive oil in a large, deep, ovenproof frying pan. Add the squabs, skin side down, and cook over medium–high heat for 4–5 minutes, or until golden underneath, then turn over and season to taste with sea salt and freshly ground black pepper.

Transfer the pan to the oven and roast the squabs for 10 minutes, or until medium–rare — the juices should still run a little pink when the thigh is pierced with a skewer. Remove from the oven and transfer to a deep ceramic or glass dish.

Wipe the frying pan clean and return to the stovetop. Heat the remaining olive oil, add the onion and carrot and sauté for 3 minutes, or until just beginning to soften. Add the remaining ingredients, bring the mixture to a simmer and cook over medium–low heat for 7–8 minutes, or until the carrot is just tender.

Pour the hot mixture over the squab and allow to cool to room temperature. Cover and refrigerate for 24 hours. Serve at room temperature.

Roast rack of venison

Serves 6–8

MARINADE
250 ml (9 fl oz/1 cup) red wine
3 tablespoons olive oil
2 tablespoons brandy
1 shallot or brown onion, finely chopped
2 garlic cloves, crushed
2 bay leaves
6 juniper berries, crushed
1 tablespoon thyme
8 whole black peppercorns

2 racks of venison (10 chops per rack)
250 ml (9 fl oz/1 cup) beef stock
1 tablespoon redcurrant jelly
2 tablespoons port
40 g (1¼ oz) butter, cut into small cubes
20 whole tinned chestnuts

Combine the marinade ingredients in a large bowl and mix well. Add the venison racks, turn to coat well, then cover and refrigerate overnight, turning occasionally.

Preheat the oven to 220°C (425°F/Gas 7). Remove the venison from the marinade and drain well, reserving the marinade. Place on a rack inside a roasting tin, then roast for 20–25 minutes for medium–rare — do not overcook venison or it will be dry and tough. Remove from the oven, cover loosely with foil and leave to rest in a warm place for 10 minutes.

Meanwhile, make the sauce. Transfer the reserved marinade to a small saucepan with the stock and bring to the boil over medium heat. Boil until reduced to 250 ml (9 fl oz/1 cup), then reduce the heat, stir in the redcurrant jelly and port and simmer gently. Add 30 g (1 oz) of the butter one cube at a time, whisking constantly with a balloon whisk to emulsify the sauce — do not add too much butter at once or the sauce will split. Remove from the heat and keep warm.

Drain the chestnuts and heat in a small saucepan with the remaining butter. Season with freshly ground black pepper.

Carve the venison racks between the bones. Divide the venison and hot chestnuts among warmed plates. Strain the warm sauce through a sieve and drizzle over the meat.

Rabbit, chorizo and olive casserole

Serves 4–6

150 g (5½ oz) French shallots
2 tablespoons olive oil
2 kg (4 lb 8 oz) rabbit pieces
2 chorizo sausages, sliced
12 baby onions
2 garlic cloves, crushed
1 teaspoon dried thyme
1 teaspoon paprika
1 tablespoon plain (all-purpose) flour
125 ml (4 fl oz/½ cup) white wine
375 ml (13 fl oz/1½ cups) chicken stock
1 tablespoon tomato paste (concentrated purée)
½ teaspoon grated orange zest
4 tablespoons orange juice
12 kalamata olives
4 tablespoons chopped flat-leaf (Italian) parsley

Preheat the oven to 180°C (350°F/Gas 4). Plunge the shallots into boiling water for 30 seconds, then drain and peel them. Set aside.

Heat half the olive oil in a large, heavy-based frying pan. Add the rabbit in batches and cook over high heat for 5–6 minutes, turning to brown all over. Transfer to a large casserole dish.

Heat the remaining oil in the pan. Add the chorizo, shallots and onions and sauté over medium heat for 7 minutes, or until the onions are soft and golden. Add the garlic, thyme and paprika and cook for 1 minute, then add the flour and cook for 30 seconds, stirring to combine.

Remove the pan from the heat, pour in the wine and stir well to loosen any bits stuck to the bottom of the pan.

Place the pan back over the heat, pour in the stock and stir until boiling. Add the tomato paste, orange zest, orange juice and rabbit pieces and mix well. Reduce the heat, cover and gently simmer for 2–2¼ hours, or until the rabbit is tender. Season to taste with sea salt and freshly ground black pepper, then stir in the olives and parsley and serve.

Venison fillets with juniper berries and red wine jus

Serves 4

RED WINE JUS
250 ml (9 fl oz/1 cup) good-quality cabernet sauvignon
250 ml (9 fl oz/1 cup) game or veal stock
8 juniper berries, crushed
2 garlic cloves, bruised
4 thyme sprigs
50 g (1 3/4 oz) butter, cut into small cubes

1 tablespoon olive oil
20 g (3/4 oz) butter
2 venison fillets, about 400 g (14 oz) each
thyme sprigs, to garnish

Preheat the oven to 200°C (400°F/Gas 6). To make the red wine jus, put the wine, stock, juniper berries, garlic and thyme sprigs in a saucepan over high heat. Bring to the boil, then reduce the heat to medium and cook for 10–12 minutes, or until the liquid has reduced by one-third.

Strain the liquid through a fine sieve and return to a clean saucepan. Place over low heat, then add the butter one cube at a time, whisking constantly with a balloon whisk to emulsify the sauce — do not add too much butter at once or the sauce will split. Remove from the heat and keep warm.

Heat the olive oil and butter in a flameproof roasting tin over high heat. When the butter has melted, add the venison fillets and cook for 8–10 minutes, turning to brown all over. Transfer to the oven and roast for 12–15 minutes, or until medium–rare — do not overcook venison or it will be dry and tough. Remove from the oven, cover loosely with foil and leave to rest in a warm place for 10 minutes.

Carve the venison into 2 cm (3/4 inch) thick slices. Divide among warmed plates, garnish with thyme sprigs and serve drizzled with the red wine jus.

Pigeon with raisins and pine nuts

Serves 4

4 pigeons or squabs
200 ml (7 fl oz) balsamic vinegar
2 tablespoons olive oil, plus extra, for brushing
1 large red onion, finely sliced
4 tablespoons pine nuts
2 garlic cloves, crushed
3 tablespoons raisins
2 rosemary sprigs, chopped
100 ml (3½ fl oz) red wine or water

Using a large, sharp knife or kitchen scissors, cut through each pigeon down either side of the backbone and discard the backbones. Turn the birds breast side up. Using the heel of your hand, press down firmly on the breastbone to flatten the birds out.

Put the pigeons in a non-metallic bowl and pour the vinegar over, making sure they are coated. Cover and refrigerate for at least 4 hours.

Heat the olive oil in a frying pan and sauté the onion and pine nuts over medium heat for 7 minutes, or until the onion is soft and transparent and the pine nuts golden brown. Add the garlic, raisins and rosemary and cook for 2 minutes, then add the reserved vinegar and wine and cook for 10 minutes. Season to taste with sea salt and freshly ground black pepper.

Meanwhile, preheat a chargrill pan or barbecue chargrill plate to medium. Drain the pigeons, reserving the vinegar. Brush the pigeons all over with olive oil, then chargrill for 5–10 minutes on each side, or until the skin is browned and the flesh cooked but still a little pink — the juices should still run a little pink when the thigh is pierced with a skewer. Place the pigeons in a warmed serving dish.

Scrape the juices from the grill pan into the sauce. Bring the sauce back to the boil and drizzle over the pigeons.

NOTE: You can also use this recipe to cook butterflied spatchcocks (poussin).

index

Published in 2008 by Murdoch Books Pty Limited
www.murdochbooks.com.au

Murdoch Books Australia
Pier 8/9
23 Hickson Road
Millers Point NSW 2000
Phone: +61 (0) 2 8220 2000
Fax: +61 (0) 2 8220 2558

Murdoch Books UK Limited
Erico House, 6th Floor
93–99 Upper Richmond Road
Putney, London SW15 2TG
Phone: +44 (0) 20 8785 5995
Fax: +44 (0) 20 8785 5985

Chief Executive: Juliet Rogers
Publishing Director: Kay Scarlett

Design Manager: Vivien Valk
Project Manager: Janine Flew
Editor: Katri Hilden
Design concept: Sarah Odgers
Design: Alex Frampton
Production: Monique Layt
Photographer: George Seper
Stylist: Marie-Helénè Clauzon (except for pages 8 and 18 and cover: styled by Sue Fairlie-Cuninghame)
Food preparation: Joanne Glynn

National Library of Australia Cataloguing-in-Publication Data

Kitchen, Leanne.
Title: The butcher / author, Leanne Kitchen.
Publisher: Sydney: Murdoch Books, 2008.
ISBN: 978 1 74196 096 9 (hbk.)
Series: Kitchen, Leanne. Butcher/Baker series
Notes: Includes index.
Subjects: Cookery (Meat)
Dewey Number: 641.66

Printed by 1010 Printing International Limited in 2008. PRINTED IN CHINA.

CONVERSION GUIDE: You may find cooking times vary depending on the oven you are using. For fan-forced ovens, as a general rule, set the oven temperature to 20°C (35°F) lower than indicated in the recipe. We have used 20 ml (4 teaspoon) tablespoon measures. If you are using a 15 ml (3 teaspoon) tablespoon, for most recipes the difference will not be noticeable. However, for recipes using baking powder, gelatine, bicarbonate of soda (baking soda), small amounts of flour and cornflour (cornstarch), add an extra teaspoon for each tablespoon specified.